Around the World
in Eight Days

Around the World
in Eight Days

The Flight of the
WINNIE MAE

Wiley Post and
Harold Gatty

FOREWORD BY WALTER J. BOYNE

•

INTRODUCTION BY WILL ROGERS

ORION BOOKS • NEW YORK

Foreword © 1989 by Crown Publishers, Inc.

Published by Orion Books, a division of Crown Publishers, Inc., 201 East 50th Street, New York, New York 10022

ORION and colophon are trademarks of Crown Publishers, Inc.

Manufactured in the United States of America

Library of Congress Cataloging-in-Publication Data

Post, Wiley, 1898–1935.
  Around the world in eight days : the flight of the Winnie Mae/by Wiley Post and Harold Gatty ; introduction by Will Rogers ; foreword by Walter Boyne.—1st ed.
    p. cm.
  Reprint, with new foreword. Originally published: New York ; Chicago : Rand, McNally, c1931.
  1. Flights around the world.   I. Gatty, Harold, 1903–1957.
II. Title.
TL721.P6A3   1989   89-3200
629.13'09—dc19   CIP

ISBN 0-517-57352-0

Design by Jake Victor Thomas

10 9 8 7 6 5 4 3 2 1

First Edition

Contents

Contents

Foreword

A little more than fifty-five years after the epic flight of Wiley Post and Harold Gatty around the world, two young Americans, Jeana Yeager and Dick Rutan, made a dramatic flight of their own in the beautiful-to-look-at but devilish-to-fly Rutan "Voyager." At first glance, one would think that the two flights really had only one thing in common: the circumnavigation of the globe. Yet, as will be shown later, there were startling similarities in the two great adventures.

For a decade the colorful Wiley Post, hair in disarray, eye patch slightly skewed, was one of the premier American pilots. Sadly, he is today virtually forgotten, his contributions vastly underrated. The reasons for this are mixed and interesting, a curious result of his own native diffidence, an inability of the public to measure the true worth of his later projects, and ironically, the fact that he died in the company of an even more famous personality, one of America's folk heroes, the comedian/cowboy/philosopher Will Rogers. Post's able navigator and coauthor, Harold Gatty, enjoyed a distinguished and varied career in aviation, both before and after their circumglobal flight. Gatty, like Post, never received appropriate acclaim for his many contributions to aviation and particularly to navigation, in which he was a seminal figure.

The public's failure to appreciate Post's later achievements probably stemmed from the press's overemphasis of his humble beginnings. It is true that Post, born in Van Zandt, Texas, but later always considered an Oklahoman, had come from poor but hardy Scotch-Irish stock. There was also some Indian blood in his ancestry so that in his wing-walking days he was billed as "The Flying Redskin." It is true that Post worked in the oil fields, and there lost an eye to a flying metal particle from a drill. It was an accident that both handicapped and enabled him, for while it cost him his normal depth perception, the insurance payment for the injury permitted him to buy an airplane.

The one-eyed Wiley Post was one of the most farseeing pilots of the time, sharing with Charles Lindbergh an ability to incorporate science into his vision of aviation. His scientific approach is evident in this book, in recounting how carefully he prepared, in whom he placed his trust, and most important, where he placed his emphasis. There is some irony that the area where he made most of his effort—control of weight and balance—would in a later flight prove to be his undoing.

As headline-making as the 1931 round-the-world flight with Gatty was, Post's later career was even more significant. He elected in 1933 to make a *solo* flight around the world. The airplane was again his famous Lockheed, the "Winnie Mae," equipped with a Sperry autopilot. This time he made the trip in 7 days, 18 hours, and 49 minutes, becoming on that one flight the first man to fly around the world solo, and the first man to make the trip twice.

At a time when interest in the stratosphere was confined to a few theorists, Post modified the "Winnie Mae" with a supercharged engine and jettisonable landing gear for high-speed flight at altitude. A special skid was incorporated on which to make semiprotected belly landings. The wooden hull of the Vega could not be pressurized to offset the effects of high-altitude flight, so he elected to have created a crude but effective full-pressure suit, a tailored substitute for a pressurized cabin. The combination worked well and permitted him to climb to altitude and use the as yet almost unknown jetstream to increase his ground speed. On March 15, 1935, he flew from Burbank, California, to Cleveland, Ohio, in 7 hours and 19 minutes, reaching speeds of 340 miles per hour.

Post's life was cut short in a tragic accident that must be considered an aberration, given the scientific bent of his previous flying. He and his friend Will Rogers (who wrote the introduction to this book) had long wanted to take a protracted flying vacation. Post created from disparate sources a hybrid, one-of-a-kind Lockheed, whose flowing lines and red-painted finish concealed two potentially fatal flaws.

Post purchased from the famous aircraft broker Charles Babb a bastard aircraft. It consisted of the wing of the Lockheed Explorer "Blue Flash," cracked up in Panama by Roy Ammel after a record flight from New York, and the fuselage of a Transcontinental and Western Lockheed Orion. Fitted with a fixed gear, the Explorer/Orion lash-up, equipped as it was with a 550-horsepower Wasp engine and a three-bladed, controllable-pitch propeller, was reasonably airworthy. Post asked Lockheed to further modify the aircraft with pontoons. Lockheed refused, revealing the first of the fatal flaws by insisting that the floats would make the aircraft so nose-heavy that a loss of power would inevitably result in a crash.

Post was tired and perhaps frustrated that his pioneering high-altitude trips had not achieved the acclaim or the financial reward they deserved. He and Rogers both wanted to make the trip, and he undoubtedly felt that his skill as a pilot could overcome the weight and balance problems imposed by the floats. In Seattle, a pair of big Edo floats were attached to the aircraft by a private firm.

It was the second, unrecognized fatal flaw that probably caused the accident. In the Explorer's fuel system (and for that matter, apparently in some other Lockheed types) at certain flight altitudes and at certain fuel loads, the flow of gasoline to the engine could be interrupted. Given the nose-heavy condition of the aircraft, even a brief loss of power on takeoff would result in a crash.

The vacation had been uneventful until on August 15, 1935, Post and Rogers made a landing on the water near the small Eskimo village of Walakpi. The two men asked natives for directions to Point Barrow, chatted with them briefly and amiably, and then took off. Post pulled the aircraft up into a steep climbing turn, the very maneuver most likely to induce fuel starvation. The engine quit, and the red plane stalled and crashed, killing both men instantly.

The nation mourned them, but not equally, for while Post was a popular figure, Will Rogers was a living legend, an important figure of films, the stage, radio, and even politics. And while Will Rogers's fame continued to grow, that of Wiley Post quietly faded away.

This sad situation should have been rectified in part by the flight of the "Voyager." The many similarities should have evoked the image of Post and Gatty, and should perhaps have resulted in a television documentary. The reissue of this book is at least a partial step in the right direction.

The similarities are genuine, and one does not have to reach too far to recognize them. Both aircraft were of advanced design for their time, and Lockheed's patented method of building a pressure-treated, plywood-molded fuselage is certainly analagous to some of the techniques used by the Rutan team. In both aircraft the dependability of the power plant and the rate of fuel consumption were critical determinants of the possibility of success.

There are other parallels. The installation of the fuel tanks and the system of fuel management were fundamentally important in the internal design of the aircraft. The disposition of the tanks dictated the location of crew members in both aircraft, and provided genuine head-aches—real and interpersonal—for both flights.

In this regard, in a very advanced bit of thinking, Post and to a lesser extent Gatty varied their sleeping and eating habits to prepare physiologically and psychologically for their flights in a regimen that clearly forecast the far more extensive training undertaken by Rutan and Yeager.

A fundamental difference, of course, was that the "Voyager's" flight was nonstop and unrefueled. The endurance requirements and the unforgiving (perhaps *frightening* would be a better word) flight characteristics of the tandem-wing airplane were uniquely demanding. Yet the stops that Post and Gatty made had their own brand of hazard—dangerous, fatigue-ridden night landings on muddy unprepared fields, refueling by jerry can and chamois with gasoline of questionable octane rating and purity, and the dreadful tendency of hosts to wish to wine and dine them. All of these things added a comparable dimension of difficulty to their flight.

Weather was equally troublesome for both aircraft. The "Winnie Mae" was naturally not so well equipped, lacking an autopilot on its first global flight and having only the standard primitive flight instruments of the day. It was, however, relatively stronger structurally in terms of its ability to withstand sudden gusts and the buffeting of storms. The pilots of the much more fragile "Voyager" could counter this to some degree by their magnificent communication and navigation equipment, and by being able to use the resources of a worldwide weather forecasting system.

But unquestionably, the most basic underlying similarity is in the courage and the capability of the two crews. The names of the team members—Wiley Post and Harold Gatty, Dick Rutan and Jeana Yeager—will always be remembered not only for their daring, endurance, and capability, but also for having the genius and determination to undertake flights that would make a permanent contribution to both the science and the legend of aviation.

Walter J. Boyne
Reston, Virginia
August 28, 1988

Introduction

Mr. Toastmaster, Post and Gatty, and Ladies and Gentlemen, We are gathered here at these bountiful tables, to do honor to two gentlemen who knew that the World was cockeyed, But wasent right sure it was round, It seems fitting that this gathering should be in Claremore, Okla. Air is these boys means of transportation, and Claremore has furnished more air to the World through one Native Son than was her share. A Man wrote a Book one time called, "Around the World in eighty days" and it was read for years, Well if these Boys after going around it in eight days, want to write a Book it ought to be read as long as prohibition will be discussed, Which means forever.

We are gethered here today to do honor to a great combination, A great Pilot, a great Navigator, a generous and modest backer, and a marvelous Plane, All gathered here to help us open our little Airport, This flight must stand out among flights of all time, Of course there was Lindbergh's—The daring, the loneliness, and the sheer skill and ability of one lone youth crossing that Ocean for the first time, No trip, no time or no history, can ever erace that flight from memory, And these two Boys would be the first to admit it, and pay honor to him, In fact I have heard them do so, But that was One trip, one dash, everything just primed for the One Big Hop, Well these Boys had One Big Hop every day and night for eight days, There is a race at Liverpool, the Grand National, almost five miles in length and about thirty of the highest and stiffest jumps in the World, When you win it, the world says, "There is a Race Horse" Well these Lads won the Grand National of the Air, and we can point to them and tell the World, "You are gazing on A Pilot, and A Navigator." The physical hardship of this trip will stand out above all others, These Birds stayed awake over seven full days out of eight, in fact they havent had any sleep yet. There must be no worse torture and misery in the World than to have to keep going, when it looks and feels like you cant possibly hold your eyes open, and how wide theirs had to be open?, We can all make some kind of a one big effort, but we cant sleep an hour and then get up and make another one just as big, and keep it up for over a week. Thats what you call a sustained effort, Well this was about the sustainingest effort that was ever sustained, They carried no Parachutes, or Rubber life boats, they simply made it or ELSE. What manner of men are these three who conceived and so carefully prepared this scheme, First the Backer, Well thats Mr Hall an Oil man, There can be two reasons for his support, One is for the pure Sportsmanship of the thing, and the other is too get his mind off the oil business, Looking at the Oil business as it is now, it was perhaps the latter, and its surprising that he dident go with them, I know it wasent the danger, for an oil man would welcome danger.

Mr Post the Pilot is another Oklahoman, He did live in Texas as a child, But even Texas children grow up, Post used to be on a Cotton farm, it wasent ambition that drove him to the air, it was the bo-weevil. If it hadent been for the bo-weevil and a Republican Administration he might have remained an underfed, overmortgaged, Farmer, So you got to quit knocking the Republicans, they really made this trip possible. He got his mechanical knowledge from working in a Garage, When people who had learned their chouffering on a Cultivator and Mule, transferred their knowledge to their first Model, T's. He had no ambition about going around the World, but he could take a wrench and go round the bolts on a Ford rim in record time, He used to work in cahoots with a fellow down at the next town, and they both learned just how to fix one of em so it would fall entirely to pieces by the time it reached the other fellows place, A Plane crashed near the Garage one day and all that was left intact was the propeller, Post took it and put it on the old Model T, in place of the fan, and took off and Solo-ed in it. Thats why away up in Siberia when the ship hit in the mud and tipped over on her nose, and did enough damage to have sent most Pilots back on the train, why he just took a hammer and some bob wire and fixed it so it added ten miles more an hour, The old garage training come in handy. He piloted the Plane on the whole trip, He was raised on a Texas "Norther" and weaned on an Oklahoma "Cyclone" So a little thing like fog looked like a clear day to him, After he had flown over seven hundred hours, the Government, (on account of what they thought was a physical iffliction) by the loss of one eye, Dident want to give him a license. Now they got men looking and offering a bonus to One Eyed Pilots, You see, the eye that he lost saw the bad weather and the bad landing fields, this one just see's the good, He is a determined looking little Rascal, and when he says quit, You can bet there would be no more Gas, or no more air.

Now this Gatty he is an Australian, Thats where they stand on their tail and kick you with their hind feet. He went to the Australian Naval College, Then when he finished he found that Australia had no Navy, He asked em about it and they told him, "Well you are a Navigator try and find it." Every Australian has to know Navigation to find where they have their Capitol located. He dicided to make a life study of Aerial Navigation, So he come to America, (Or the U.S. Rather, for there are other America's,) He said to himself, "There is a country with more air, and nobody knows where they are going, so it ought to offer a Navigator a chance," I know if I was a Navigator, there is lots of people that I see wandering around in public office that I would go offer my services too just for patriotic reasons, He can take an $1.00 Ingersol Watch, A Woolworth Compass, and a Lantern, and at twelve oclock at night he can tell you just how many miles the American Farmer is away from the Poor House. He can look at the Northern Star and a Southern Democrat and tell you if Oklahoma will go Republican, or sane. He knows the Moon like a Lobbyist knows the Senators, Give him one peek at the Giant Dipper, the 86th Meridian, and the Northampton, Mass, Mail carriers bag, and he can tell you if Calvin will run again. He allied himself with this wonderful Pilot Post, and they made this marvelous record, but it would have been worth a lot more, if he had joined Mr Hoover, as a Navigator, He has had more fog and tough weather ever since he took off than Post ever saw. He has scraped his landing gear on many a mountain top. There has been times when even a Wickersham Report would look almost like clear weather. Gatty had a compartment in the back of the Plane where he couldent see Post, He is the only back seat Driver that ever made good, There was times when he had nothing to take his bearings by but a Russians Whiskers. He would see which way they was blowing, and the velocity, to get his drift from.

It will be a long time before their record is broke, for it will be a long time before there is such an ideal combination of Pilot and Navigator, We want to thank both our foreign Neighbors, Australia and Oklahoma for loaning the U. S. these two fine Boys. Its payment in a way for us loaning Mr Kingsford Smith a great Navigator on his marvelous trip to Australia, which will stand out among flights for all time. That was a great combination too, When you hit one of those tiny Islands in the Pacific, you have got to have more than a Lincoln Highway Road Map. Ah! But the marvelous thing about all the flights is the Modesty of the men who do them, And these Boys have carried on that tradition to a T. Not a boast, Not a speck of Egotism, We are fortunate with our Heroe's, Ever since these Boys have been back they havent made a wrong move, They deserve all they can legitimately derive from the trip, Gosh what a chance they took, and with what percision and determination and skill they carried it through, No American begrudges them what little return they will derive on their tremendous investment.

Now the Wives, Here they sit enjoying a fleeing bit of addulation, But who were the real Heroe's of this trip? Wasent it them, Dident their bravery in letting The Boys go make it possible,? What do you think they did through those eight days?, How much did they sleep?, The person doing the thing gets the constant thrill, But the one waiting only gets the grief, So it took more than Mr Hall with his generosity, Mr Post with his skill, Mr Gatty with his knowledge, and Mr Somebody with his round World to bring this about, No behind it all it took the sacrifice and courage of two Women, So lets give a Toast to Mrs Gatty and Mrs Post and the Wives of every Flyer, For they are the Heroe's.

Will Rogers

Part One

Preparation

HOW IT ALL BEGAN
AND WHY

(POST)

I DON'T REMEMBER EVER HEARING MUCH ABOUT MAGELLAN when I was a kid, and even the Cabots are pretty dim recollections, but I still get a kick out of my old history book which shows a picture of Columbus looking out to sea. Columbus thought he was going around the world to Asia, and just that phrase "going around the world" had a great thrill for me, especially as my view of the world was the flat horizon of Texas.

I think that was the spark which, fanned by a spirit of adventure, set me planning, in the autumn of 1930, a flight around the world. Cross-country flying had become monotonous to me, and the steady grind of piloting my employer, F. C. Hall, from one bad landing field surrounded by oil derricks to another, was beginning to wear on my spirit.

When I joined Mr. Hall as his personal pilot, we had an understanding to the effect that I would be free to make special flights in the interests of aviation or for my own amusement. I had just won the nonstop derby for men in

9

the National Air Races, and with it a purse of $7,500. Returning to my home field at Oklahoma City, I found that the general business depression had encroached on the stronghold of the oil drillers. Expansion programs of the Hall interests were being held back. Business in flying was dull, and I faced the prospect of several months' idleness unless I could find some way out for myself.

With various plans in view, I appraised the situation. I felt that the time had arrived to take advantage of Mr. Hall's promises. Aviation needed something original to stimulate passenger business. The impetus, begun in 1927, had resulted in the nation's being covered by elaborate networks of air lines. But there was still the bugaboo of the flying hazard, and the public needed more definite proof of the reliability of the airplane under all conditions.

A glance at the map revealed that most of the fields of the flyer's endeavor had been conquered and well conquered. The two coasts of the United States had been brought within 12½ hours of each other. Frank Hawks had been able to shrink intercity distances almost to the vanishing point. The refueling fad had proved conclusively that modern airplanes will fly indefinitely if given fuel. North, south, east, and west, almost every possible flight had been made. There remained the oceans. But flying oceans, since Lindbergh, Chamberlin, Coste, and the others had conquered the Atlantic, seemed unnecessarily hazardous. In addition, it would prove nothing that was not already an established fact.

However, at the 1930 races in Chicago, the promotors of dirigibles and lighter-than-air machines had challenged the supremacy of the airplane.

The European dirigible, the "Graf Zeppelin," had landed in Lakehurst, New Jersey, just 21 days, 7 hours and 34 minutes after it had soared into the air and nosed out from the same port. It had circumnavigated the globe. It had done what Columbus might have accomplished, had he not bumped into the North American continent on the way. It had reduced the time taken by Magellan, the first globe-circler, by more than 3 years. Because of its long record of service, the "Zeppelin" was rapidly overshadowing the airplane in the public mind from the standpoint of safety.

Looking at the log of the huge and, to my mind, lumbering airship, I was convinced that that type of transportation would never supersede other forms of air transport. Speed has been the keynote of all transportation developments since the beginning of the wheel-and-axle days. Safety has been more or less secondary to speed. But even from the safety standpoint, the airplane had a remarkable record in American aëronautics. The occasional accidents had been much overemphasized, and later investigations by aëronautical experts had revealed that nearly 90 per cent of these accidents could have been prevented.

So, for one with a cautious disposition, and with a reasonable amount of experience in flying, there was nothing to fear from the airplane.

Pilots with unusual records were being made into heroes. I think these men would be the first to deny being any more "heroic" than the average pilot. They were just doing what they set out to do. They knew how to do it and they succeeded. It was as simple as that. The so-called "superhuman qualities" were, in their own estimations, nothing more than myths.

What I was ready and anxious to prove was that a good airplane with average equipment and careful flying could outdo the "Graf Zeppelin," or any other similar aircraft, at every turn on a flight around the world.

My equipment consisted of one airplane, the fastest load-carrier I had ever seen, and the promised backing of Mr. Hall, in addition to the few thousand dollars I had

saved. On the personal side, I had had seven years' training in flying, mostly of the hardest sort. I knew from past
experience a navigator who could chart a course for me so
that I could almost follow it accurately without a map. This
navigator was Harold Gatty. He had plotted the 1,760-mile
course I had just flown to win the nonstop derby for men.
His charts were so accurate that even when my compass
broke when I was halfway through the long run, I had
held the plane true and beat my nearest rival by more than
30 minutes in a 10-hour flight.

Mr. Hall needed very little persuasion to give not only
his permission to use his plane, but his active support to
the initial preparations. He made only one condition. That
was, that no commercial interests should be enlisted.

"Whatever profits, if any, result from the flight, will be
used to defray the expenses, and you will have to hope for
a surplus for remuneration," he said.

That condition puzzled me. If there were no commercial
dealings, how were there to be any profits? I finally got
him to agree to my enlisting several concerns of the aircraft
industry, provided they did not capitalize directly on the
flight itself. I also won his permission to sell the running
story of the flight to a newspaper. But he insisted that I
was to refuse to give any personal endorsements on equipment or merchandise—at least until after the flight was
made and his part of the bargain was fulfilled.

This was a serious handicap to getting under way. Hard
work had taught me the full value of money, and I hesitated before spending any great amount on so idealistic a
venture, particularly when I knew that so many business
men were ready and anxious to deal with me. They were
spending enormous amounts annually in other forms of
advertising, and what seemed a great deal to me was but
a little to them.

After thinking it over for nearly a week, I flew to Los

Angeles to talk with Gatty, whose coöperation was so necessary to the flight. He had several theories of aërial
navigation which he was anxious to try out, and just as I
had figured, he looked on the proposed flight as an ideal
opportunity to do this. I knew then that Mr. Hall would
find a strong ally in Harold Gatty and so I agreed to his
condition, although I realized preparations for the flight,
without commercial backing, would involve much personal labor and some delay.

As I afterward found out, half the satisfaction of accom-
plishment lies in anticipation and the hard work of
preparation. Gatty and I went to work with a will. Together we went over all the plans that I had previously
considered when I had thought of competing in a nonstop
flight from the United States to Hongkong. He reviewed
with me all the data he had collected on his unsuccessful
attempt to fly the Pacific with Harold Bromley during the
summer of 1930, when storms and fog turned them back
to Japan after they had covered a great part of their route.

I found that Harold knew a great deal in regard to landing fields and conditions in the Orient, northeastern
Siberia, and Alaska, in addition to having collected much
meteorological information for those areas. In fact, I was
so impressed with his vast store of geographical and meteorological knowledge that I felt free to leave that side of
the preparation to him and to devote all my time to the
practical engineering and mechanical end of the flight.

So I left Gatty to his books and his students in his navigation school at Los Angeles and returned to Oklahoma
City where, for the next few months, my work was comparatively easy. Part of it was training my mind and body
for the long grind ahead. I didn't want to take any chances
of causing delays on the flight because of physical inca-
pacity or mental fatigue.

As I flew about the country in the regular routine of my

job, I tried my best to keep my mind a total blank. That may sound easy, but it is one of the hardest things I ever had to do. According to my theory, it was of primary importance in overcoming one of the greatest dangers on the flight—slowed-up reactions at the end of a long hop. These might easily result in ground-looping or some other form of minor accident in landing.

By keeping my mind a blank, I do not mean that I paid no attention to the business of handling the ship. I mean that I did it automatically, without mental effort, letting my actions be wholly controlled by my subconscious mind. I am not a psychologist by any stretch of the imagination, but I have analyzed some of the events leading up to bad landings after long flights. I have seen pilots who are numbered among the best "stick technicians" in the country plop their planes down, when they were tired, so that only the good turf on the airport saved them from breaking something. Those landings were perfectly safe, of course, but as Gatty and I were not going to carry any spares on the trip, one broken shock absorber or blown tire in the far reaches of Siberia might mean a month's delay and the failure of our plan to break the record.

Another thing I had to learn was to control my sleep. I knew that the variance in time as we progressed would bring on acute fatigue if I were used to regular hours. So, for the greater part of the winter before the flight, I never slept during the same hours on any two days in the same week. Breaking oneself of such common habits as regular sleeping hours is far more difficult than flying an airplane!

Other habits also had to be regulated in accordance with my special home-made course in physical and mental training. I found one interesting thing. By limiting my diet, I could get along without much sleep. Several times Mrs. Post accused me of trying to reduce. She said, "If your margin is so small that the few pounds you take off by dieting mean so much, I don't think much of your chances of getting through."

I smile now when I think about it. All my irregular living was upsetting her regular household routine, and of the two of us she went through the greater ordeal.

Meanwhile we were charting the way. Gatty sent me a tentative outline of the route he thought we should follow, and asked me to go over it carefully from the standpoint of the limitations set by the airplane.

That brought us to the second stage of the preparation, a long one, filled with much calculation. We had plenty of data from past flights, but most of these flights had been made under better-than-average conditions. We could hardly expect to find even average conditions on the complete circle of the world. So we had to arrange our route to allow a little leeway in case of slight delay.

It took a long time to gather information by mail and cable from the remoter places over which our route lay. While we waited, I took the ship to Los Angeles to have its tanks revamped and its details altered to fit it for the unusual flight conditions it would have to stand.

2

THE "WINNIE MAE" MAKES READY

(POST)

My training in irregular habits, or in the complete lack of habits, continued up to January, 1931, when I picked up stakes in Chickasha, Oklahoma, and headed west with the "Winnie Mae" to put her in shipshape condition at the Lockheed factory in Los Angeles. I felt a bit apprehensive. This was the first step on my greatest adventure. I knew that I would feel almost at home in the old plant where I had once been a test pilot and general utility man, but I could not help wondering just how the whole thing would come out.

Mrs. Post was with me. We had closed our apartment and attended to the usual details that people about to go on a vacation attend to.

When I started out from Chickasha, I made one bad mistake which forcibly illustrates how careless pilots can get through overconfidence. The extra tanks, which I had removed from the cabin after the 1930 nonstop derby to make room for the seats, were just thrown into the back along with our luggage and whatever tools and gadgets I thought

I might need at Los Angeles. The inside of the ship was an awful mess, and quick exit was practically impossible for Mrs. Post, who rode amid all the confusion.

As we taxied out to the runway, the tanks made a terrific amount of clatter, and I was afraid that some spark might be generated from the friction. Although they had had no gas in them for months, it was unsafe to take such chances. However, nothing happened. The guiding spirit which I hoped might be our mascot in the final dash seemed to be with us then—but through no fault of mine. I resolved to pay more attention to details in the future.

When we arrived at Los Angeles, I immediately got in touch with Gatty and he outlined his plan. I had him make up a list of all he would need in the way of instruments, luggage, and other supplies for the trip. I needed every bit of information I could get before I laid out the plan of loading the plane and started placing the fuel tanks and balancing the ship so that it could be properly trimmed for flying at its maximum speed.

Of course, the load of the ship was to vary. Whatever we carried in the way of personal belongings and permanent equipment would be constant, while the great fuel load would lighten as the flight progressed. If we put too much of the constant load in the nose and balanced it with fuel behind the center of gravity, our plane would get nose heavy as soon as we ran low in gasoline. The same thing applied to loading the tail.

I knew I would need at least 500 gallons of fuel to make the longest hop on the proposed route, some 2,550 miles according to the first plan. Even that did not leave much leeway in case head winds held us back, so I tried hard to figure some way to get in a few more gallons.

The collecting and compiling of all that information was a long job and one of many compromises. Not the least of our problems involved the system of communication between Gatty and myself. The total loading of the plane and the computing of graphs to show fuel consumption per hour, per mile, and according to the speed of the motor had been eliminated in my plan. From my own experiences with the "Winnie Mae," I was quite sure without further tests what the ship would lift, and how long and far it would fly.

The main part of the work, then, rested in redesigning the interior. The problem necessitated close coöperation from Gatty. During my very first interviews with him I had found him so willing to work with me, even to the point of sacrificing and inconveniencing himself, that immediately we got off on the right foot together. Probably that factor had more to do with easing the work along to a good end than anything else.

The ship was a standard Vega model such as had been used on commercial air-transport lines and by private interests for carrying six people at high speeds. To make the picture complete, I might outline the specifications of the ship. It has an over-all length, from the hub of the propeller to the trailing edge of the rudder, of 27 feet, 7½ inches. The span of the wing is 41 feet, and the cord is tapered. The height is 8 feet, 10 inches. The general construction is of plywood with metal fittings and internal wood bracing.

The type is known to the trade as a "high wing, internally-braced cantilever monoplane, with monocoque fuselage in plywood." Translated into everyday English, this means that the wing is mounted above the fuselage. No struts or braces hold it in place except those within its own covering, thus leaving no appendages to interfere with the smooth flow of air. The monocoque construction of the fuselage means that the body of the plane depends for its strength on its own tubular shape, and that the internal ribs of the cabin are run only laterally in order to maintain that cigar shape. No longitudinal members are in the cabin except the flooring, which does not extend all the way.

In regard to the rest of the plane detail, part was of my own design or adaptation. The Pratt & Whitney motor in the nose is known as the "Wasp" model. It was equipped with a military-type supercharger with an impeller, or blower, running ten times as fast as the engine in order to force the fuel vapor from the carburetor into the manifolds of the intake system at a pressure. The commercial-type Wasp has a similar arrangement but with the impeller operating at a ratio of seven to one. The stepping up of the ratio increases the horsepower of the engine by nearly a hundred, but the hourly consumption of fuel also increases in greater proportion, so that the mean equation traces a delicate line when dealing with maximum loads and speeds. With the blower at ten to one—a combination I had used on the Los Angeles-Chicago race equipment and later had removed—the engine could develop more than 510 horsepower at 2,200 revolutions a minute and would furnish a 150-mile-an-hour cruising speed with an hourly consumption of 22 gallons at 1,700 revolutions. On those figures I arranged my fueling and time schedule, allowing a reasonable amount for adverse winds.

When I brought the ship into Los Angeles, I turned the engine over to the Pratt & Whitney Service Department for a complete overhauling. I also tightened the structure of the plane itself in all the vital corners wherever any sort of routine service was needed.

I decided to leave the wings at the angle at which I had formerly set them—a lower incidence than they originally had—having no doubt that I could get my load into the air with that setting and without too long a run at any of the airports from which the heaviest loads were to be taken.

Then came the problem of loading the fuselage. I didn't like that part of the work, so I have avoided talking too much about it thus far!

So many things can happen to airplanes that are badly loaded. A tail-heavy plane, flying through the air with its elevator and stabilizer set at maximum nose-down position, more or less has the tendency to "mush" along with undue lifting forces exerted on the wing and tail surfaces. This increases the resistance offered by the air and slows the ship down, increasing correspondingly its fuel consumption. The reverse situation—a nose-heavy plane—while better than tail-heaviness, still wears the pilot out, and sets up undue strains on the top side of the horizontal tail empennage.

It was up to me as pilot of the "Winnie Mae" to get the last ounce of available efficiency from her. I figured on loading up so that I would not dare put on an extra five pounds. My calculations had to be accurate, for I was not going to run any advance tests.

I knew from the way the ship had handled on the trip from Los Angeles to Chicago in the National Air Races that the center of gravity was just right for that load. But I wanted more fuel and I had a navigator and a more constant weight to carry on this flight around the world. If I put the constant weight directly on the center of gravity where it would make the least difference, I would be all right. But, small as Gatty was, he couldn't fit where only a fly could ride. Then, if I put him ahead of the "c.g.," I would have to carry the fuel behind, and as soon as the gasoline load grew light, the ship would need a lot of trimming to keep it from growing nose heavy. Landings with an empty tail, a tired pilot, and a 75-mile speed are the best reasons why the propeller companies are sure of doing a big replacement business.

All this detail seems very technical, but it played an important part in our plans. With help from the engineers at the factory and using the ingenious speaking-tube system recommended by Gatty, we finally managed to accommodate the full load so that, light or heavily laden with fuel, the ship would fly on an even keel with only a slight change in the stabilizer setting. Gatty's quarters behind the tanks were far from comfortable but he unhesitatingly agreed to put up with them. Some comment was caused by the fact that his chair was not held to the floor. That was due to a slight tendency of the ship to bounce on the tail in fast landings when lightly loaded. Harold had to move forward or back in his two feet of leeway, depending on whether I was trying to hold the tail up or get it down. That shows how delicately the ship had to be balanced, as under ordinary conditions so slight a shift in the position of so light a man would hardly be noticed by the pilot. His moving forward was even more of a help in getting the tail up with the heavy load of gas than his backward motion was in holding it down when we were landing.

All these changes cost Mr. Hall the N C license, issued by the Department of Commerce, which permits the carrying of passengers. The ship had to be put through with an N R license, which is a restricted license for special flights and which forbids the carrying of passengers as long as there are extra gasoline tanks on board. The rules of the Department of Commerce are rigidly enforced with regard to N R licenses, so the owner of the craft could no longer fly in the "Winnie Mae."

The navigational preparations and equipment can be explained much better by Gatty, so I will confine myself to my own end of the ship up in the stuffy little cockpit. Banked off from the cabin by the tanks which extended to the sides and top of the fuselage, I had to enter and leave through the trapdoor on the roof. I was completely cut off from the rear. I faced one danger, however; in case of a nose-up landing, the tanks might break loose from their anchors and fall on me. Once that happened, it would never happen again!

The interior of the cockpit was all fixed up to my taste, and it is a good thing that comfort was the word. I replaced the customary straight-backed, steel "bucket" with a nice roomy armchair. It was a trifle short for leg room perhaps, but quite restful. I had plenty of room to shift positions without getting too far from the controls. Of course, my purpose was to keep from getting stiff during the 20 or more hours' cruising range. In ordinary flying it is not necessary to sit in one position so long, but this time I was to make precision flight over the course the keynote of my piloting so that I could get the last mile out of my fuel and the best speed toward the record.

Then to equip the instrument board. The motor instruments gave me little or no worry. I would put them anywhere so that they could be seen. I knew my engine and had no fear that it would need the slightest attention in flight.

I had talked with some of the pilots who had flown planes to Hawaii or to Europe. They were all of the opinion that a great part of the chance for success rested on the location of the flying instruments. Weather reports are weather reports, but when out in the middle of the ocean, a pilot must be prepared to meet almost any emergency. There is no field out there to sit down on and wait for a fog to burn itself away in the sun. While it is true that there are no buildings or mountains to run into, it is often most difficult to keep an airplane flying on an even keel.

My claims to "blind-flying" experience were limited to three or four isolated instances. When darkness shut in around the plane and it got so black one might as well have been looking up through the inside of a derby hat, my only procedure to date had been to turn and run into the first clear spot, sit down, and wait until I could get through. On those few occasions I might have flown blind for as long as 20 minutes at a time, but my sensations were most uncomfortable, and, I must admit, the thing was dangerous.

It was on the advice of flyers like Jimmie Doolittle (who visited the plant while I was getting the "Winnie Mae" ready), Roger Williams, and others who had proven their ability to fly blind over long stretches, that I grouped three flying instruments so that my eyes and other senses coördinated best. They were the bank-and-turn indicator, the rate-of-climb meter, and the artificial gyroscopic horizon.

The first of these three instruments runs but a fraction of a second behind the plane in its reports. Each slight gyration of the plane is shown on a swinging hand which flops in the direction the plane is turning. The hand works in conjunction with a regular bank indicator, which lets the steel ball in a glass race slide up or down on the bank to show a sideslip in or a skid out if the plane banks too far or too little, respectively.

The rate-of-climb meter is most valuable in blind flying. Contrary to popular belief, an airplane does not always fly true to the angle at which its longitudinal axis is inclined. I have held the nose of a plane down in rising currents of the invisible medium through which we fly, and have gained several hundred feet of altitude in the short space of a few seconds. These air currents, or "bumps" as we call them, travel in both directions, up and down, and might easily throw a ship, being flown blind, off balance or into the water, without warning.

Last, but most important in my set of three instruments, was the artificial horizon. This instrument has a tiny cutout of an airplane mounted in the center of its dial. A white line across the face represents the horizon. The instrument is connected to a small gyroscope which resists change in direction. The white line across the face keeps in line with the flywheel of the gyroscope, so that when the plane tips in any direction, the change is immediately shown by its position in relation to the model airplane which, of course, remains fixed on the center of the dial.

Under normal conditions in smooth air, the artificial horizon is an inclinometer, a bank indicator, and a rate-of-climb meter all rolled into one. But in rough air the other two instruments tell a more accurate story, not of the plane's position in relation to the horizon, but of its direction of travel with regard to the earth.

The compass, of course, had to be set so that it could be seen with equal facility. For our flight we installed compasses of the aperiodic type, developed first in England, which do not oscillate as violently as the flotation-type magnetic compasses.

Then there were the instruments customarily found in most transport planes—an air-speed indicator, a tachometer for telling the engine speed, fuel gauges, oil-temperature and cylinder-head temperature dials, and instruments showing pressures of oil and fuel feeds and other details of motor conditions.

Not the least important was the air-temperature indicator. This was more than a thermometer. It warned us when we were flying through air where there was danger of ice forming on the wings. Ice formation is liable to occur at temperatures ranging between 40° and 33° Fahrenheit, when the moisture content of the air is sufficiently high for precipitation against the cold wing. When the wing gets well below the freezing point of water, the ice will not adhere to it. This eliminates the danger of colder levels.

Any error in flying under conditions where the formation of ice is possible usually proves disastrous. The ice "spoils" the air about the wing, detracting from its lifting qualities in addition to adding greatly to the weight of the plane.

Eastertide found me ready and anxious to go. The "Winnie Mae" was washed and polished, had had a good rest and a thorough overhauling, and was "all set." I knew without test flights what her limitations were, and how far her strength and endurance could be relied upon, with careful and loving handling.

During the process of preparing the plane, Harold Gatty and I had had a series of conferences. Now I was anxious to learn how his preparations in planning and plotting the course were progressing. I felt that we ought to get away with the first change of moon in the summer season—the time when records showed most favorable weather for flying eastward over the Atlantic.

Harold had arranged the schedule of fueling points from the data I had given him on the range of the ship, and a good job he had done so far as I could tell from my hearsay knowledge of European and Siberian airports. He was so thorough that he even communicated, as far as possible, with the managers at the scheduled landing fields.

But I am getting away from my end of the ship. Harold had better tell about his work, himself.

DRIVING FROM THE BACK SEAT

(GATTY)

WHEN WILEY POST, THE MAN WHO WAS GOING TO BE MY helmsman on a voyage around the world, dropped in at Lindbergh Field, California, on January 17, 1931, and told me the time was ripe to prepare his airplane "Winnie Mae" for her dash after the record of the "Graf Zeppelin," he found me busy teaching my small class of navigation students and tutoring a few transport pilots who were interested in learning how to find their several ways through strange lands without maps.

All my life I had been seeking adventure and twice I had thought it was to become realization. Once, when I went to sea—but after eleven years I found that the life of a ship's officer is to the adventurer's soul what flat beer is to the epicure. And again, when I climbed into the cockpit of Harold Bromley's airplane at Tokyo and headed east over the Pacific for the United States. The experience was destined never to become full adventure, as fog and a faltering engine forced us back after we were well on the way across the ocean and our goal seemed attainable.

I went home after seeing Wiley, and began making plans to fix my affairs so that my wife and three children would be taken care of while I was gone. I had an assistant at the school of navigation who was capable of taking care of my students, and the backer of the flight, F. C. Hall, promised to see that my home would be taken care of in case the school did not adequately provide for it.

Twenty-four hours later I had forgotten everything but Post and his "Winnie Mae." I journeyed to the Lockheed factory for an inventory of the present assets of our plan and immediately began adding to them.

I found Wiley in deep discussion with a plant engineer over some of the changes he wanted made in the airplane. He and the engineer went over the ship, from her gleaming propeller to the fan-like flippers which regulated her direction at the tail. I saw that Wiley had very definite ideas as to how his plane should be, and I began making my own plans as thorough as his, so that we should not become lost, regardless of what flying conditions we found on our way.

My first thought was of navigation, of course, and where and why we should put the "bridge and chart room" of the good ship "Winnie Mae."

To sail the plane while Wiley flew it, I had to be in a position to see up and ahead, and down and behind. There were other details—how much weight I would be allowed to carry, and the exact location of my seat with respect to the center of gravity—but those matters were of little concern to me.

The matter of where I was to ride was taken up by Wiley at the first instant when I became *of* and not merely *in* the plan. He installed my chair and table behind the big fuel tank and ordered two hatches built, one overhead and just forward from my seat, and the other on the bottom of the yacht-white, cigar-shaped cabin. Through the first I was to "shoot the sun" (or stars), and through the other I was to calculate the drift and ground speed of the plane. With those two "eyes," the "Winnie Mae" could find her way anywhere if the laws which regulate this universe of ours held constant for the duration of the flight.

For the benefit of those who do not understand the theory of navigation by celestial observation, or the computing of courses by dead reckoning when clouds prevent sight of sun or stars, I shall point out a few of the rudimentary rules which guide the mariner over uncharted or unmapped areas of the globe.

Time and distance as we know them on the surface of the earth are one and the same quantity to the navigator. Distance may be expressed not only in miles, as we measure it in ordinary life, but also in time; that is, the distance between two points may be measured by the length of time required by the sun to pass from one point to the other, or for it to assume with respect to the second point the same position that it held at a given instant with respect to the first.

For instance, take Dresden, Germany, which lies in the same relation to the 15th meridian east from Greenwich as London does from the Greenwich or zero meridian. We can tell from our map just how far it is in miles from London to Dresden, but to the mariner, the distance is one hour, or 15°, or one twenty-fourth of the time it takes for the earth to rotate once to expose each of the cities at the same inclination to the sun.

In the reverse process, we find that by knowing the altitude of the sun above the horizon, as seen from our position, we can compute our distance in time from any point on the earth's surface for which the same information is known. Greenwich, the zero meridian, has been adopted as the standard for such calculation and Greenwich civil time is therefore used as standard. The variance between Greenwich and exact local time is therefore equal to the distance which separates the two points. By local time I do not mean the time as set by zones, with subdivisions only into hours, but the time apparent by observation of the sun, stars, or moon with divisions into minutes and seconds.

The process shown above will accurately determine the time-distance of any point east or west from Greenwich, but will not show the exact distance in latitude between the two points. But the inclination of the sun from all points on the equator is known, and by a similar observation we can determine our latitude from the equator. Knowing latitude and longitude, we "fix" our position at the point of intersection between the latitude parallel and the longitude meridian represented by the figures computed from the observation.

So much for the outline of navigation by celestial observation through the roof of the cabin. Now for the hatch in the bottom through which the drift indicator may be focused.

I prepared a special drift-and-speed indicator for the flight around the world in which only one known factor was required, namely, the altitude above the object sighted.

Anyone who has ever ridden along the bank of a river knows how different the apparent speed is between the near and far banks. By mechanical means my drift indicator reproduces such an optical illusion, and from the reading of the instrument I can tell exactly how much the plane has drifted in a specified time or how fast it is traveling. The instrument is somewhat similar in appearance to a microscope. In construction, it is similar to the projection outlet of a motion-picture machine. The eyepiece can be moved closer to or farther from the spectrum through which a film moves at a constant speed, governed by clockwork.

The procedure for making observations through the indicator is as follows. We estimate, or fly down and measure upward, our exact altitude from a spot on the surface of the earth. When aloft, I focus the eyepiece on it and start the clockwork going. There will be a difference in the apparent speed of the film and the rate at which the spot is passing across the spectrum, so the eyepiece is moved until both speeds apparently are equal. A table which I have prepared to go with the instrument shows the ground speed for the two known factors of the observation: the distance of the eyepiece from the film, and the altitude of the instrument from the object sighted.

For drift, the operation is simultaneous with that for calculating speed. In normal position the center line of the spectrum runs along the longitudinal axis of the plane. If there is any side motion, that is, if the plane is "crabbing" along, blown by a cross wind, the object sighted will not move along the center line. The indicator is then turned until the motion of the ground is parallel with that line. At the end of the observation the number of degrees which the instrument had to be turned from the true axis of the plane indicates the angle of drift.

The uses of the first of these two navigational processes are obvious. If we can get continual observations, our course can be accurately determined. But when clouds obscure the sky, no observations can be made. Then it is that the navigator resorts to "dead reckoning."

Dead reckoning is a problem in geometry, although in its close refinements it becomes spherical trigonometry. But for amateurs, geometry will do.

For illustration, let us undertake a flight between New York and Boston, 201 miles air line with a true course 63°

from true north. As we take off from Newark Airport, imagine our predicament when we find it is so hazy that we cannot follow the landmarks shown by the map. The navigator then determines his speed and drift. He also knows the various details which affect the compass along the way. With one calculation he can find the course which the plane must follow to hold a true course of 63° and from his speed he knows almost to the minute what time Boston should pass beneath. The various details affecting compasses are taken up in the story of the actual flight across the ocean. They are variation, deviation, and drift, and on the imaginary flight between New York and Boston might be found to have quantities of 14° west, 2° east, and 5° left, respectively.

That means that our course by dead reckoning would include the following data. To the true course of 63° we would add the 14° our compass swings to the west of true north due to the magnetic variation of the earth in this zone during 1931. This would make our magnetic course steering 77°. Now a former test in compensating the compass may have revealed that in our airplane the magnetic attraction of the metal in the ship made the compass swing 2° to the east when reading between 45° and 90°. Those two degrees must therefore be subtracted from the 77°, which will make our course 75°. With the drift at 5° left established, we will have to alter the course to 80° before we can expect to fly over Boston without having a further check on the course en route. And to do that, the drift will have to remain constant throughout the flight, a condition over which we have no control. Within certain limits this form of dead reckoning is accurate enough for ordinary flying over short distances. It is shown here so that the preparations for the flight around the world may be better understood.

For each leg of the flight I made up charts and plotted

courses from every bit of data I could collect in those four months of preparation. Of necessity I had to leave out the drift and speed calculations, for I had no advance information in which direction or at what speed the winds would blow. But I did know that in still air at 150 miles an hour we could start out from Harbor Grace, or any other one of the stops, and fly a definite magnetic course for a specified time before we altered our course to suit a new set of still-air conditions. The gaps and discrepancies between still-air and actual-flight conditions were thus the only calculations which had to be fitted into the navigational scheme en route. The equipment for celestial observation was put in so that we could have a constant check on the course we were following even when at sea, where we had no landmarks to get our exact position otherwise.

To gather the maps and information on terrain, airports, airport facilities, and other details of the flight was part of my job in preparation. Wiley was kept busy fixing the airplane so that it would accommodate the fuel load and the personnel and would fly at the cruising speed of the navigational charts. It was a long and arduous task to prepare both plane and route on paper, then in test, for so long a flight.

At last the "Winnie Mae" was put together, motor and all, and we decided to test out our equipment on the flight east to Washington, D.C., where we had to obtain permission through the embassies of the countries over which we intended to fly. Our quarters were not very comfortable, but we would not have to endure their discomforts any longer than the minimum time it would take "Winnie Mae" to go from point to point along the way, and our speed was great. Our original schedule of ten days, in which we hoped to complete the flight, ought to permit our taking time out to rest, we thought, and still allow us to set a record for our around-the-world flight ten days better than that of the "Graf Zeppelin."

With our preparations complete we shoved off from Los Angeles on May 17, 1931, and landed in Oklahoma City the next day. I left my family behind. Mrs. Gatty and the children were enthusiastic in their encouragement, although the little ones hardly knew what it was all about.

Mrs. Post, herself an air enthusiast who has flown many miles with her husband, was also most encouraging. She helped with the arrangements in the plane and gave her advice to Wiley on many matters which expedited our start for the Atlantic seaboard. She joined Wiley's family in Oklahoma to await with them our return.

Mr. Hall, who had journeyed several times to Los Angeles to aid in the preparations from the standpoint of the backer of the flight, now left his business in Oklahoma City and went by train with his daughter, Mrs. Winnie Mae Fain, and her husband, to New York where he stayed with us for a week.

When we arrived in Washington, D.C., we called on the diplomatic representatives of Great Britain, The Netherlands, Germany, Poland, China, and Japan for permission to fly over or land within the boundaries of those countries or their possessions. The envoys were all solicitous in our behalf and gave us instructions and letters which would aid us materially en route. We did not plan to land in either China or Japan but obtained permission to do so in case weather forced us that far off our course.

So, armed with passports and permission from our own State Department, we landed at Roosevelt Field, May 23, with but two things lacking—good weather, and official permission from the authorities of the U. S. S. R. to visit their country. Through the Amtorg Trading Corporation in New York we received assurance that the Union of Socialistic Soviet Republics would not deter us from making the flight through their domain but could not give us any official recognition. The Soviet Government, however, did everything in its power to aid us under the circumstances, and that portion of the flight, which took us more than a third of our way, would have been much more difficult if it had not been for the unofficial coöperation of the Soviets.

ON THE MARK—
GET SET

(GATTY)

NONE OF THE TRIALS WE HAD DURING OUR SIX MONTHS OF preparation was as great as the long days and nights of waiting to take off from Roosevelt Field. When we landed there, our enthusiasm was at its highest pitch. Daily we approached the final test of our plan. But as the weeks wore on, the continued bad-weather reports from distant and watery spots on the relentless North Atlantic wore us thin with impatience, and we soon developed that nervous tension which comes from enforced idleness and delayed anticipation.

We felt the "Winnie Mae" might develop lazy habits if we let her idle much longer. Dust collected on her nice white skin, and I began to check and recheck the instruments just to have something to do with my time.

Wiley had a few new dials, including the Sperry Horizon, put on his instrument board, and spent hours on end in the office of Dr. James H. Kimball, the guardian angel, guiding spirit, and foster father of flyers who take it upon themselves to dare the ocean. From the meteorologist's office on top of the Whitehall Building overlooking the Battery and Upper New York Bay, Wiley's good eye looked out with alternate longing and anger. Stoical in the face of bad weather, the Statue of Liberty remained adamant to his pleadings for her to turn to the northeast and cast her beam over the Great Circle Course.

We soon began to weary of the extreme caution advised by our associates. We knew that we could not possibly have favorable weather throughout an around-the-world journey, and we could not see what difference it made over which part we took the bad weather.

It was Dr. Kimball who dissuaded us from starting a week earlier than we did. The charts of the ocean then showed weather about as clear as that which faced us when we at last took off. The winds were not as favorable, but that made little difference to us as long as they were moderate. The extremely high cruising speed of the plane prevented our having to wait for tail winds.

We gathered in Dr. Kimball's office for a council of war. We pointed out that our route was but of 16 or 17 hours' duration over the fog and storm-infested areas on his current chart, and that Wiley's ability to fly blind through clouds and fog would carry us through.

To this the benevolent weather man smiled with that characteristic patience for which he is noted. Standing by his drawing board, Dr. Kimball gently reproved us for our belligerent attitude toward the deadly enemy:

"I have seen a great many of you lads who dare the ocean to do its worst," he said. "Only those with blind-flying ability have succeeded, and then it has been only by virtue of every other aid in wind and weather.

"I am ready to admit that your plane is faster and therefore not as subject to disaster from head winds. You may get through an area of blind fog in half to three-quarters the time the slower planes must take, but you will still have a long, hard grind ahead. It will not do to wear yourselves out on the first leg of the journey.

"Now, if you look at this chart, you will see that fog, head wind, and cold hang over the Grand Bank and extend about 500 miles to sea. To battle through that—what with danger of ice formation on your wings, a heavy load of gas, no way to check your course at the start from Harbor Grace, and other hardships in the way of overcast skies and head winds—is almost beyond human endurance. I have great respect for your courage, but in my experience I have noticed a sharp division between the judicious application of courage and the foolhardiness of overconfidence.

"So why not be sensible about it? The weather must sooner or later improve. It may not permit the slower ships' taking off, but it will surely give you two more than a 75-per-cent chance where now you have less than a 50-per-cent chance of ever getting four hours out from the coast."

It sounded like good advice. That was my first trip to the daily conferences the learned scientist and Wiley had been holding for several weeks, and I felt the hypnotic influence of the meteorologist's quiet but businesslike manner. I was glad I had been there, because I knew even better than Wiley what fog is at sea and how it makes the most seasoned mariners cautious. We decided to talk it over with Mr. Hall, who was still at the Hotel Biltmore.

Going back through the maze of skyscrapers, we passed the Empire State Building. The 1,250-foot tower was lost in the overhang of the clouds. I shuddered to think what might happen to the "Winnie Mae" if she were rushing through that overhang at 170 or 180 miles an hour. I pointed out the possibility of that sort of disaster to Wiley, but he only smiled.

"Well, you'd know how high it was before you got

there," he said. "Allowing for a good error in the altimeter and even an error in your navigation, we could still give it a wide berth."

Nevertheless, I made up my mind then and there to be a restraining influence on Wiley's enthusiastic optimism.

From the windows of the Biltmore I pointed out a similar phenomenon to Mr. Hall and made a strong ally in him. The nonchalance, tempered with ability and a knowledge of its limits, which makes Wiley the pilot that he is, was much misunderstood by both Mr. Hall and myself at that time. I had a few misgivings of my own ability, for I had never quite forgotten a certain night watch at sea when I had stood on the bridge and blindly groped my ship's way across Cook Strait, New Zealand.

With sobriety dampening our enthusiasm somewhat, we held another conference the next morning in Dr. Kimball's office. The day was clear and cool, and we agreed not to try a start until he gave the word that the fog area was less than an hour's run in thickness. That and the semifrigid atmosphere near Newfoundland were the only two things which had to be dissipated from the weather map before we could begin our dash.

But sea weather grew steadily worse. The first moon of the summer waned with storms raging on the ocean. Several times steamers were delayed by dense fogs. Right in New York Bay several minor collisions occurred.

Meanwhile, a whole troupe of prospective transatlantic flyers was assembling at the various flying fields around the city. They were all waiting for the same thing—good weather—and Dr. Kimball was the busiest man in town. The chief topic of conversation around the hangar was ocean flights, and there was a lot of speculation on the chances of the various expeditions. Planes destined to carry much heavier fuel loads in proportion to their speed and power than the "Winnie Mae" were almost constantly in the air, trying out their equipment on long series of test flights.

It was about this time that we made our one and only test. I was walking through the hangar and just happened by the "Winnie Mae" when I noticed that the compass in the back compartment was pointing north by west. I knew the plane was headed about northeast as it stood. Checking with the compasses on other ships and the one in the front cockpit of our own plane, I found that there was an error of nearly 45°. I looked around for some strong magnet or other cause for such deviation, but couldn't find any.

I had to check our compasses in the air, anyhow, and Wiley thought that would be a good time to do it, so we made a test flight and got both compasses checked.

We also recalibrated all the other instruments to such precision that we had to change several of our charts on which we had allowed for known errors by marking out the dial readings over specified sections of the route. This was almost a superfluous move because, once known, the errors were more or less constant, and could easily be allowed for in flight readings. But it gave us something to do and helped stave off the boredom which came from our enforced idleness.

The moon, reaching its last quarter on June 8, found us still tense and waiting. As the first quarter of the new cycle peeped out of the east shortly after midnight on June 16, our spirits rose. A general change in the weather seemed to forecast our early departure.

We packed up our belongings and moved from the Biltmore Hotel, where we had been staying, out to the hotel inside the field gate. Mr. Hall was summoned back to Oklahoma to attend to his oil business. All our bills were paid, and gas was waiting for us all along the line. We snatched sleep between the weather reports which we received three or four times each day from Dr. Kimball's office. We were ready for a take-off on half an hour's notice at any time during the next week.

At last Dr. Kimball furnished us with a chart. We reflected on the time we wanted to start. We figured that we ought to get away from Roosevelt just before dawn, land in Harbor Grace in the forenoon, and get away within two hours for Europe. We calculated our speed with the wind velocities shown on the chart, and estimated that we should land in Berlin in the early evening light the next night. Tempelhof, the Berlin airport, was well lighted, but we wanted to make sure that we could see to land in case our fuel ran low during the last hour or two.

"Winnie Mae" was gassed and her smooth white skin wiped off. Wiley kept the wire busy almost constantly telephoning to Dr. Kimball. Colonel Lindbergh called up and wished us Godspeed. Everything looked like a "go" on that morning of June 20.

But, no! The anticlimax was still to come. A storm was racing east from the Hudson Bay district. We faced the danger of getting as far as Harbor Grace and not being able to see the airport. The weather data from northern Quebec were hard to gather as observatories are few and far between up there.

We got out at midnight. Dr. Kimball telephoned, informing us that he had a lot of long-distance calls in for New Brunswick and would not know the exact progress of the storm until 2 o'clock. We felt that we just had to beat that storm through.

We couldn't afford to take any chances of delay at Harbor Grace, because our elapsed time was to begin as our wheels left the ground at Roosevelt Field. The others who were waiting to fly the ocean could go to Harbor Grace and wait for good weather, but that would spoil our chances for a record flight.

The storm beat us to the take-off that time, and nobody

benefited except the 'phone company. Plunged in gloom, we went back to bed with bitter thoughts. The storm, we thought, would go on out and be checked by the Gulf Stream. That would leave it raging off the Grand Bank, bringing on bad winds and possibly heavy fogs where it hit the warmer currents of air.

But instead, it hovered over Newfoundland and Labrador. We hoped momentarily for word that Harbor Grace would report visibility conditions good enough for us to land. We rearranged our schedule so that we could start with the first news of clear weather there. We hoped to land, refuel, and take off again in time to beat the storm to the Gulf Stream. Its travel east would help us along, even if we did have to fly through it with a heavy load and with no sight.

As if it were sent to plague us, that blot on the map moved up and down the coast of Newfoundland. It seemed even to center its activities at Harbor Grace. We made rough calculations on landing at St. John, New Brunswick, instead, but the hop from there to Berlin was too much for our fuel load. The runway at St. John was pretty short, too, and we didn't dare try to take off with the full load.

The next night we tried again, but with no better luck. We lost a lot of sleep that day, what with reporters waking us to ask if we were going, and with keeping in constant touch with the weather bureau.

On June 22 we heard that things were getting better up at Harbor Grace. By 11 P.M. the visibility was more than a half mile, the ceiling was about 500 feet, and a fresh wind from the southwest was rapidly pushing the storm northeast and out of our path.

At midnight we decided that if the weather got no worse, we would go. We fixed 3 A.M. for our take-off. Feverish haste accompanied our last-minute preparations.

Again the load of sandwiches. Again the arrangement for a final call to Dr. Kimball.

A slow drizzling rain set in at Roosevelt Field. By 2:30 A.M. it began to rain in earnest, and we feared the slippery, soft field on unit No. 1 where hard-surfaced runways had not been built. The previous day we had taxied the ship over to this field from field No. 2, where our plane had been in storage.

We were dressed in the only suits we had left. Wiley had taken our light ones to the cleaners in Mineola, and they were not ready. We commissioned Bill Ulbrich, a pilot at Roosevelt, to get them for us and have them ready for our return. Wiley had a note scribbled in Russian from the woman who ran the cleaning shop and had promised her to give it to some one at "Moskva."

The endless posing for photographers tired us. The eerie light effects from the calcium flares were almost blinding, and the acrid smoke from them hung low in the damp air and rain. It was stifling. The airport lights danced in the prisms they made through the sheets of rain which increased every minute. Wiley called Dr. Kimball and found that he had learned the weather at Harbor Grace was still on the mend.

Of all the excitement in the dingy old buildings around the old part of the field I think that which made my own coat heave was the greatest. I found myself trying to memorize figures and charts which I already knew by heart.

Calm old Wiley! He plunged through the rain in a borrowed raincoat. One would have thought he was going to take Mr. Hall off on a 100-mile hop and had lots of time.

The zero hour came. I saw so many times indicated on the four chronometers that I had to use a pencil to convert Greenwich civil, sidereal, and eastern standard times before I realized that it was 3 o'clock.

Then Wiley used his head. With that rain it would have been impossible to be sure on the take-off. Looking through the diamond-like drops on the windshield at the brilliant lights of the airport would distort everything. He refused to risk our months of effort on a few drops of rain and a few seconds of rushing along the ground at 70 miles an hour.

He said we would wait for dawn, which was 2 hours away on the daylight-saving plan. Greenwich civil, the time I was going to use throughout the flight, said it was 7:14 A.M. in England, The day was Tuesday, and I made a note of that. From that point on we were going to have trouble with our memories in regard to days of the week.

We fled from the pelting raindrops into the old shed. A small group of friends followed us: Bill Ulbrich, Viola Gentry, Russell Boardman and his partner John Polando (who were soon to follow us in a Bellanca), Walter Ward of the National Aëronautic Association, who was to be official timer for the record, and some of the reporters and photographers with whom we had struck up friendships. To add to the excitement, Herb McCrory, a photographer, got a bad burn from a flash-light powder which exploded prematurely in his hand.

In another 12 hours it would have been a month to the hour since we had landed at Roosevelt Field, ready to go. It had been a long wait, and the time had dragged, but during that last 2 hours before the dawn of June 23 it didn't seem long at all as we looked back at it. Our friends encouraged us, and we grew calm, or at least I did—Wiley had been tranquil all along.

We even sat down and counted out our money. Wiley had $34, and I had what the old vaudeville joke calls "some money." That $35 was to last us until we got back, and we were going around the world. Things were not as bad as that sounds, however, for all the bills and supplies for the plane had been paid for in advance and our hotel accommodations arranged.

It seemed as if the rain would never stop. As the first gray streaks came over Westbury, it poured down worse than ever; like a resounding wail it screamed against the roof of the shed.

I was calm enough to remember the *Polite Conversation* of Swift. In answer to the question put to Wiley as to whether or not he would postpone the flight, I interjected:

" 'I know Sir John will go, though he was sure it would rain cats and dogs.' "

Wiley, in his soaked clothing, was particularly unimpressive as Sir John, but his efficiency was not impaired. With the first sight of dawn on the horizon, he strode out to the ship. He squinted into the tail and found that a quantity of rain had seeped through the hatch above my seat and settled near the vent. If he hadn't had presence of mind enough to drain it out near the tail skid, I would have been treated to a good shower bath on the take-off when the tail rose.

We shook hands last with Dick Blythe, who with his partner, Harry Bruno, was acting as our personal representative. All set to go, we stood by.

After posing one last time for sound-news men, we climbed into the ship. From my compartment aft I heard Wiley's cheery and sharp "Gas on; switch off," and the reply from the mechanic, "Contact!" was so sharp that it rang in my ears even after the low roar of the engine started.

We taxied off to the northeast corner of the field, over the rough hummocks of slippery, wetted grass. I watched the streamliners on the wheels slice their way through the waving reeds.

I sucked in my breath as Wiley gave the Wasp all the

throttle it could take. Friends, field, and fences swept by the tiny windows as we flashed along the runway. One bounce, a second lighter one, and the plane hit the last with a heave and bounded into the air.

I turned to my little table, picked up my log book and pencil, and made the first notation. It was a nice black book, and I had all my tables ruled in red on the back pages.

On page 1, under the heading "New York—Harbor Grace," I added:

"Tuesday, June 23."

And in the first column, under "G. c. t." (Greenwich civil time), I made the entry:

"8:55:21."

In the last column, under "Remarks," I wrote:

"Took off 4:55 daylight-saving time, set course 63°, visibility poor."

Part Two

The Flight

5

JUNE 23

FROM NEW YORK TO HARBOR GRACE

(POST)

THE CLOCK ON THE INSTRUMENT BOARD SHOWED THAT IT lacked 5 minutes, maybe a fraction less, of being 5 A.M. when I pulled the "Winnie Mae" back on her tail at Roosevelt Field. The grass was wet, and I was relieved that no side gust hit us as we plunged along. I wouldn't have dared to use the brakes.

The stout old wing mushed along for 100 feet without pulling the ship off. A hard hummock hit the right wheel and flexed the shock absorber to its limit. A rut sent the plane bounding into the air, but it settled back with a light bounce.

Suddenly, as the air-speed needle hit 80, the stick became rigid and sensitive to my touch. From its mushing position the wing pitched to a higher angle, and I moved forward a little to hold the ship down. The wheels spun idly, and I could see, through the rain, the eaves of the white hangars and the flashing track of the propeller. The red roof of the Air Associates hangar, which had been the home of the "Winnie Mae" for a month, swept underneath, and Mineola was just ahead. I started a turn, a nice shallow bank, and below us the Long Island Railroad tracks and the bungalows of Mineola circled past the windshield from left to right. Through the side window appeared Carle Place and the hangar in which we had waited 2 hours for light.

"Doc" Kimball had said we would run into clearing weather, but it looked pretty black ahead to the northeast. Just then my thoughts were interrupted by Harold at the other end of the speaking tube.

"Set your course at 63° and stand by till we get it right," he said.

With a slow motion, so as not to set the compass in oscillation, I shoved my right foot forward a quarter of an inch at a time.

"A little more to the right," came through the tube as the steer point reached 60°.

I was holding the ship down to 400 feet to keep the ground in sight. At our speed the rain made visibility bad. I could see it running down the windshield and along the motor ring. It was a rather gloomy morning to be starting out to fulfill a great ambition.

With the compass resting comfortably on 63°, I settled back to the business of flying the "Winnie Mae" to what I hoped would be a decisive victory over the record set by the "Graf Zeppelin." The arms on the big chair I had put in the cockpit seemed to yawn with me as I tipped back. I began to wish that I could get some altitude that would let me forget the stick and fly the ship on the stabilizer and rudder. But at 400 feet, things happen too fast for one to let go of the stick.

I didn't pay much attention to things as they slipped away below. I noticed the Fairchild plant at Farmingdale "going by" on the right. Next I saw the big estates beyond Huntington. Then the little village of Northport marked the spot where we were to leave Long Island.

As Northport came up in front through the right window, I dropped down over the edge of town, and we headed across Long Island Sound for Connecticut. We were making knots, as the sailors say, and the water clipped by in a hurry. I guess we flew so close to it that Harold, sitting in the back with no forward view, must have been a bit worried, because he shouted through the speaking tube:

"You ought to get up a little higher. We might run into the lighthouse on Falkner Island. It should be right ahead."

Just to ease his mind, I wound down a bit on the stabilizer and pulled up over a boat. It must have been one of the Boston boats headed for New York that the night run through the rain had made a little late.

I picked up the Connecticut shore line in a couple of minutes while the plane was still in the slight climb. We flew over land again—the marches and redstone hills just east of New Haven. For a while the shore line lay right on our course, but not for more than 5 minutes, and by the time we passed it off our trail, we had about 1,500 feet. It was broad daylight now, and I got one glimpse of the Hammonasset River.

"Cut over a little more to the right," I heard Harold say through the tube. "We're making only 138 miles."

"That's because we're climbing," I shouted back. "How are you getting on?"

"I never felt better in my life, thank you, Mr. Post," he said, "but cut a little more to the right."

A little more pressure on the right foot and the horizon swung almost unnoticeably across to the left of the nose. I caught sight of a factory with the name "Guilford, Conn." written across the roof. The clock said 5:24, so we must have been going about half an hour.

We climbed steadily for the next few minutes, and at 2,000 feet I wound the stabilizer back up to level off. The air speed jumped to 150 miles an hour, and the motor picked up a few revolutions without my touching the throttle. The old Wasp was ticking it off and singing a sweet song in my ears.

It was too much trouble to talk back and forth over the tube, so I didn't try to keep Gatty entertained with my conversation.

"We are picking up speed," was his next remark at 5:50, and from the sound of his voice I knew he was munching on the sandwiches he had insisted on bringing. "You ought to be picking up Woonsocket in a minute."

I have to hand it to him for that remark. He hardly had finished speaking when a town came up ahead. In a couple of minutes we went right over it, and on a big red roof I read "Woonsocket." I knew Harold couldn't see anything up front, so that accurate spotting of location gave me plenty of confidence that we wouldn't get lost while he was navigating the ship.

For my part, I might as well have been in a strange land. I had flown over New England only once in my life and that had been two years before, in the 1929 National Air Tour. At that time I had gone from Portland, Maine, to Springfield, Massachusetts, but since I was flying along with a fleet of planes I hadn't paid much attention to the scenery.

Hardly had the hands of the clock passed 6, when houses appeared. We were picking up the outskirts of Boston. At 6:07 I could see the East Boston Airport off to the right. The weather was getting better all the time. We had run out of the rain, and although the sky was still overcast, the ceiling was about 2,500 feet and the visibility was good.

"Change your course to 38°," Gatty called, still eating, to judge from the sound.

I swung slowly to the left and pointed the nose of the ship directly along a road which ran as straight as a string.

We followed that road for exactly 13 minutes, and it brought us out right over Newburyport. On the road we saw the first signs of life. Automobiles crept along it. Perhaps they were hitting a mile a minute, but to us they seemed to creep.

Newburyport was a sleepy-looking place so early in the morning. I remembered meeting a mayor from there on the 1929 tour. He hadn't been sleepy, by any means.

We lost the road there and headed right on, without veering to right or to left, for another 25 minutes or so. I knew we were making fast time because, before I could say "Jack Robinson," we passed over the Navy Yard at Portsmouth and along past the beach resorts of Maine.

Portland hove into sight, and when we got over the center of the town, Gatty had me change the course again to due east, 90°.

"Hey! We don't want to go out over the ocean from here," I called back to him.

"You won't," he answered. "Just keep on going and leave the course to me."

I never knew there was so much water between Maine and Nova Scotia. I had heard of the Bay of Fundy, but it had always looked so small on the map.

We lost sight of Portland about 7 o'clock, and 15 minutes later Gatty told me to steer 82°. That made me feel better. The next thing I heard was:

"We are running into a quartering wind. Better swing 4° to the left. Steer about 78°."

We held that course for the next 3 hours. For the first 2 we saw nothing but water, a few tiny wooded islands, wholly isolated and seemingly deserted, and one small fishing boat. Two men in it waved at us enthusiastically, but we were past the boat so fast that I didn't even get a good look at it.

Our first sight of foreign territory came when we picked

up the west shore of Nova Scotia. We were then right down over the water of Minas Channel, and the first town we sighted was Baxter Harbour. We ran on over the narrow neck which stretches toward New Brunswick. When we passed the irregular rocky shore and bays at Pictou, we shot out over Cape Percy and skirted the rocky coast of Northumberland Strait, which separates Nova Scotia from Prince Edward Island.

By this time, I was getting anxious to arrive at Harbor Grace, so I plugged forward a little on the throttle and stepped the "Winnie Mae" up to 180—just about full out. The motor roared as if it could feel its own progress, and the prop simply bored a hole in that air. As we hit over the neck of land on the north side of Nova Scotia, we were squat down over the deserted countryside and the noise of the motor increased, due to its reverberation against the rocky soil.

We were crabbing right along with the horizon drifting from right to left when Harold shouted through the tube as we headed out over St. George Bay toward Cape Breton Island:

"Better hold her 10° or 11° more to the left. We don't want to miss Newfoundland and get headed out to sea. We are 'way ahead of schedule. We've been making better than 175 miles ground speed for the last 2 hours."

I steered round to 65° and opened up. We were kicking a lot of air behind us and had only a little way to go. I was beginning to feel a bit hungry, too. The weather was only fair, and I wanted to be sure to get away from Harbor Grace before it had any chance to shut in on us.

I picked up Grande Miquelon Island, a tiny French colony off the southeast coast of Newfoundland, at exactly 11 o'clock. The French fisherfolk ran out of their queer-looking little homes at the approach of the ship, and

Harold told me later that as we passed they ran back in again, as if in fear.

Then St. Johns and the main part of the hooklike peninsula on the east side of Newfoundland came up through the right window. That was a blessed sight to me. I could almost smell the lunch I was going to have. After a last 50 miles over points and bays with funny-sounding names, which we slid by in nothing flat, I got my first sight of the runway at Harbor Grace.

The airport is located back from the fiord, on the one comparatively level spot in that barren, rocky land. Just to the north is Lady Lake with an evergreen forest on the far shore, which gives the lake the appearance of a huge eye fringed with beautiful lashes.

Fred Kohler had picked out the runway site back in 1927. It was with their traditional capacity for hard work that the Newfoundlanders cleared it of stumps and boulders and scraped it almost entirely by hand. The 4,000-foot path stretches toward the prevailing westerly wind. Coming in, planes have to drop over a rocky bluff and land with a downhill roll, but after 2,000 feet the runway slopes uphill. Just beyond the end, the ground rises rapidly.

I circled once and then steered out over the bay. The Wasp hushed as "Winnie Mae" turned her nose down toward the field, and I yanked back the throttle.

"Get as far back toward the tail as you can, kid," I shouted through the tube.

I could feel Harold shift his weight aft as I wound the stabilizer all the way back to hold the nose up and the tail down. I brought the ship in over the hill in a straight glide. Then I slipped her down on the left wing and gave the motor about 800 "rev's" on the throttle. That's the safest way to land on such a field. Tail down, I pulled her up to an angle near the stalling point and worked the throttle against the braking effect of the wing as it mushed through the air. We lost our altitude slowly and then touched as I closed the throttle and rolled almost up to the gas drums, where a comparatively tiny group was waiting. Our flight didn't seem to excite these folks a bit. They were used to seeing aviators bound for a European destination.

We jumped out quickly and made for food. Some photographers wanted to take our time with a lot of posing but we asked them to wait until after lunch. They deserved the picture. They had come all the way from New York, taking 5½ days by ordinary means of travel to get there, while we had made it in 6 hours and 47 minutes.

The first person to greet us was Herman Archibald, a tall white-haired man with youthful, energetic steps. He strode out, megaphone in hand, followed by three or four children representing a family of twelve young Archibalds.

Herman's brother-in-law, Mike Hays, was the official greeter of the town. He had his car there to take us in for luncheon. Mike runs a taxi daily over seventy miles of rocky road to St. Johns and uses his spare time to greet flyers and cover take-offs.

We cleared the customs men quickly, and Mike drove us down to the Cochrane House, run by Herman's sister, Rose Archibald. There we found a hot meal waiting for us.

Those Harbor Grace people took things seriously. While we ate, Herman kept three wires busy collecting weather reports for us, and the local forecasters, whose weather predictions are based on rule of thumb and tradition, squinted into the sky.

We found that aviation isn't just a stunt up there. The crazy flyers who leave there for Europe are, to those people, definite forerunners of a transportation system to England that will place Harbor Grace on the map. The movement to develop the airport has been aided by the neighboring communities of Carbonear, Spaniards Bay,

Brigus (the home of Captain Bob Bartlett), and the entire east coast of the island settlement.

Herman told us the history of the place. In his quick, clipped Newfoundland speech he stated that the people there believe with utmost faith that aviation is to be the salvation of a dying community. Not so many years ago Conception Bay was continually filled with a hundred or more ships. Whalers, ore boats, and fishing schooners did a lot of business in Harbor Grace in bygone days, but now the blue bay is dotted only by a scant sail or two, and the people are in hard straits.

I would like to have heard more, but time was pressing on and we had a long way to go. So I said good-by to Rose, and we drove back to the airport, where Ted Carlyle, the mechanic from the Pratt & Whitney plant, was supervising the gassing of the "Winnie Mae."

When we arrived on the field, the crowd was larger, and the police had staked off the area around the plane. I pitched in to help Ted. Gatty got out his charts and, using the tail of the ship for a table, he calculated the time elements in his position-charting, so that his work would be easier after we took off.

Just then two men, Holger Hoiriis and his passenger, Otto Hillig, broke through the crowd. Hoiriis, a long, lean fellow, asked me if I needed anything. He offered to send his mechanic over to help, but we didn't have much left to do then. Mr. Hillig, who owned the Bellanca they had with them, didn't say much. We four posed for pictures together. Hoiriis said that they would follow us across next morning. His "mech" was giving the Bellanca its last testing.

The weather was much warmer than I had expected. It was just 60° by the "Winnie Mae's" thermometer when I started my round of inspecting the ship. Mike Hays was talking to Hoiriis and Hillig, and Gatty was still working on his charts. As soon as I had finished my inspection, we said good-by to everybody and climbed aboard. It wouldn't do to waste much time in prolonged leave-taking.

JUNE 23–24

HARBOR GRACE TO CHESTER

(GATTY)

WILEY SAID AT LUNCH AT THE COCHRANE HOUSE THAT THE flight from Roosevelt Field to Harbor Grace was "just an ordinary trip" for the "Winnie Mae." His words were music to my ears. The 6 hours and 47 minutes for that run meant that, if we kept up that average speed, we ought to cross the ocean from land to land in about 14 hours.

We were going to have a lot of dirty weather, though, and we knew it. While Wiley might be able to fly when he could see nothing beyond the propeller and wing tips, I had never yet learned to get a look at stars or the moon when they were hidden behind clouds and fog. That made navigation guesswork, at best.

My chronometer said it was 15:42 when we landed at Harbor Grace. That was Greenwich civil time and 4 hours ahead of New York daylight. The ship was gassed and looked over while we ate, and we had it loaded to the gunwales, as it were, with fuel and other things. I went flat broke in Harbor Grace, buying sandwiches. I spent my one and only "buck" and had to be dependent on the bounty of Wiley from there on.

Wiley had implicit faith in the "Winnie Mae" and in his ability to handle her tricky moods. I had had a sample of some of them on the way to Harbor Grace when the rough air bounced us around off the Maine coast. My little table was crowded with delicate instruments, and what with figuring out the drift and speed and holding things down so they wouldn't break, I was a busy man. But the swiftness of the ship more than made up for whatever inconvenience I was put to.

I was the one to whom the ocean flight meant so much. To Wiley, it was just incidental to a trip around the world. But I had a lot of theories of aërial navigation to test out, and my reputation with my associates in aviation on the Pacific Coast depended on the results.

After our lunch at the Cochrane House, accompanied by interesting tales of Newfoundland from the Archibald family, we went back to the airport. There we met Hoiriis and Hillig. I had a nice talk with them and we exchanged good wishes.

Wiley was the most amazing person. Within sight of the "Winnie Mae," he became a different man. I shall always remember his moves at Harbor Grace as one of the high lights of the race. Despite his calmness, I have never seen him so meticulous.

The ship was ready when we walked over from the car. Wiley climbed up under the wing and drained the water traps himself. He checked and found that 540 gallons of fuel were loaded. Ted Carlyle insisted on pulling the cowling off to check the valves, but Wiley was just as positive that the engine didn't need it.

"She's running like a watch," he said, "and when you've as tough a job as this to do, it is good policy to leave well enough alone."

His attitude was not like that with the rest of the plane, however, and he made a close inspection of the ship. With maddening thoroughness he moved about, but the precision of his movements inspired confidence in me as I watched. Not a motion was wasted and not a square inch of the vital parts of the "Winnie Mae" escaped his inspection. With borrowed pliers he tightened fuel couplings, tested vents, and got oil all over himself, so that he looked like a "grease-monkey" when he finally stood on the spat of the wheel for a last pose in front of the suppliant photographers. Then his head disappeared into the cockpit, and he started the engine.

He spent fully 10 minutes warming up and testing. First on one magneto and then on the other, the motor ran wide out. When both "mags" were turned on and the throttle pushed full ahead, the terrific roar of that exhaust echoed and reëchoed throughout the rocky barrens. The "Winnie Mae" strained against her brakes, and her tail fluttered madly in the hurricane set up by the slipstream. Holding the stick back against his belt buckle to keep the tail down, and with both feet jammed hard on the brake pedals, Wiley let the motor roar out its defiance to the 1,900 miles or more of open water which lay beyond the tranquil harbor. He cocked his one good ear to the tune of the exhaust, and his one good eye was glued to the tachometer. No drop in revolutions showed on the indicator as the tail pipes of the exhaust spat out long tongues of blue flame which licked at the white paint behind the cowling ring.

Satisfied at last, he nodded to me, and I scrambled in excitedly. The biggest moment in my life had arrived. I was about to fly over the ocean. I could not but think what my former shipmates would say about my idea of crossing the Atlantic in one night.

All the details of our stop and preparations at Harbor Grace had taken 3 hours and 43 minutes of our valuable time. It was then 3:25 P.M. in New York, and we were 1,153 miles from our starting point. Including the stop, we had averaged a little better speed than 100 miles an hour, which meant that over our entire route, 17,000 miles by the longest track we contemplated, we should get through in about 170 hours—only 2 hours more than a week. It was too much to hope for; to complete the trip in that time we needed every possible amount of luck. However, the law of averages was more in our favor with each increase in our speed. The less time we spent making the flight, the less chance we had to encounter setbacks and the more time we could afford to lose in case some minor mishap did delay us a few hours.

As I peeped from the window, the scene was perfect. One could scarcely imagine a wilder or more beautiful spot. The homes and churches of Harbor Grace dotted the steep hillside that extends down to the black deep waters of Conception Bay. Across the short span of water more rugged hills rose. Beyond, lay Cape St. Francis and the heights of Belle Isle, where the largest iron mine in Newfoundland is located.

That was all I had time to see. Wiley opened the motor again in a last test as the plane faced into the wind on the far end, where the little group was waiting to watch us go.

And go we did! Wiley let the brakes loose. We headed slightly cross wind. By the time we had gone 100 yards, the "Winnie Mae" was already lightening on her landing gear. We left the ground just as we came to the rise in the runway, so I knew we had gone about 2,000 feet. I clicked the hand of my stop watch and made an entry in the log:
"Took off 19:25—wind northwest."
The little gathering on the field dropped rapidly from view, and we veered to the right as Wiley made a wide flat turn over the lake. We hung low over the land, and it

seemed as if the spruces were streaking uncomfortably close to the wheels.

With a 180° turn we headed back on our tracks at about 800-feet altitude. I picked out a spot and focused my ground-speed indicator on it to get a quick check on the wind velocity while there was still a stationary mark to see. I heard Wiley pull the throttle back to cruising speed and in a few seconds found that we were making 170 miles an hour. That meant 20 miles of help each hour from the wind.

The land dropped away sharply as we flew over the town. In the bay, a lone rusty-looking ore boat was slowly plodding its way toward Belle Isle. We passed St. Francis Point, the last headland, and nosed out over the sea, steering 89°.

Just then I saw a warning signal. A bit of white, like steam, floated above the headland and stood out against the brown cliff. Fog, low hanging! It looked as if we were on the edge of a low-pressure area. I knew we were in for it, but I had not expected it so soon.

The sky was slightly overcast, but I managed to get in a couple of sights. At 20 o'clock (4 P.M. daylight time in New York) I located at 48° 10′ N. Lat. and 51° 25′ W. Long. That showed a slight drift to the right, so I allowed 5° and passed the word through the tube to Wiley to alter his course to 84°.

The problems of figuring out courses on the sea while one is moving so rapidly are far too technical to be set down here, so I will try to explain just the important points without going into the calculations.

In the first place, the variation—the amount of change in the magnetic influence of the earth on the compass—runs high in some of the areas off the Grand Bank and has to be allowed for in the computation of the magnetic course to be followed. Another compass error, deviation, which is the amount of influence the metal in the airplane exerts on the compass, also has to be taken into account.

The earth being round, in circling it we have to follow a track which is really an arc, although one sitting on the moon directly over our course would see it as a straight line. To follow that track, however, requires constant changes in course to compensate for the variables in the navigation equations.

The airplane and dirigible, because of operation in three dimensions, further complicate the equation. This has an important bearing on aërial navigation because of the changes in the apparent elevation of the sun or stars, which must be considered in computing lines of position from these bodies.

Aside from those points, we still have three main items to know before we can arrange the course. They are speed, drift, and exact location.

Many years of research have produced tables which give the exact locations of stars, sun, and moon at every minute of the 24 hours in each of the 365 days of the year. They all pass through regular cycles of time and space, and by the use of a standard time their position-charting may be reversed, so that taking the positions charted for them as fact, we may locate our own exact position on the earth.

Of course, I had all the changes in course figured out before I started on the trip. But with no knowledge of what winds would prevail, or at what altitude we were going to fly, and with no advance check on our ground speed, I had to make observations every half hour on that flight through the night. For these I used three instruments: a sextant, a drift indicator, and a ground-speed indicator. The sextant is an instrument for measuring the vertical arc between the horizon and a star, or other celestial body. To make sure of the time, I carried three chronometers, because a minute of error in time meant a 15-mile error on the equator in the final calculation of position.

I also used a special series of star curves of progression compiled some time earlier by Commander P. V. H. Weems and myself. By using the chart I eliminated the necessity for long mathematical computations which would have told me, on completion, only the position I had been in before I started the plotting.

This fixing of position was a serious business with me and kept me busy during most of the flight. When sights were not available, I had to keep rapid check on the course Wiley took and to instruct him from a graph made up from dead reckoning, on which the course was figured according to the last known limits of error and the known amounts of variation over the course to be followed.

I had the route arranged beforehand and had 15 positions which we should cross marked out on the chart. Each half hour I would try for a sight en route and then check with the chart to see how near we were to the position we were supposed to pass at that time. The 15 marks were each about 200 miles apart.

We reached position 2, 48° 59' N. and 50° W. at 20:25 o'clock (subtract one hour for each 15° west from Greenwich to the zone in which you live to find what time it was then in your home—the hours above 12 show afternoon) and we were flying at 500 feet through low-hanging fringes of clouds and the hazy damp air of early evening. A sight warned me that we were drifting south of the course, and I told Wiley to allow for a 9° error and keep left. He pulled the ship up to 1,800 feet to try the clouds for a possible ceiling then and everything disappeared. The dense vapors swirled about the plane and seeped in through the cracks around the door.

Just about this time I remembered the radio aboard and my promise to send out signals every hour. I didn't know much about radio and didn't have much time to fool with it. I did jiggle the little key a few times, but in asking about it after we landed, we could not discover that anybody had heard the signals. We carried the set mostly as an emergency measure in case we needed to lead a ship to our position.

Turning from the radio, I tried to look out. It was just as if somebody had pasted up the window with a gray material. The dim little light in the cabin threw a ghastly orange glow over everything, and shadows danced in the corners.

We dropped down then and from 1,600-feet altitude could just about see the black carpet below which should have been the water. It was getting dark under the clouds, and I put out the light to improve my chances of seeing things outside.

"Are you all right?" I asked anxiously through the tube.

"Sure. We are making good time, aren't we?" came back a strange voice. At least in that blackness out there it sounded strange, coming as if from nowhere above the thunderous roar of the engine into that tiny cabin.

"I can't tell now because I haven't had a chance to get a sight," I replied.

"Well, let's stick it out down here and go by dead reckoning as long as we can't see where we are going," Wiley sent back. From the tone of his voice he wasn't a bit worried, I thought, but for myself, I would have been much more comfortable on the bridge of a steamer.

I would have given a lot for a fleeting shot at the sky then, so I kept the sextant handy. At 21:55 o'clock I got about 10 minutes in at the setting sun and found we were right on the course, still making 170 miles an hour, and had just passed position 3 at 50° 43' N. and 45° W. We had covered about 425 miles since leaving Harbor Grace, and we plunged on into the black night.

The variation changed at that time to 32° W. and I called to Wiley to alter the course to allow for that and for an extra 3° for the drift, as the winds were now out of the south-southwest, blowing us northward 12 points off the port bow.

That made the steer course 97°. We followed that figure on the compass dial for the next hour. At the half-hour mark I had nothing to sight and no indications which might denote a change in conditions, so I told Wiley to keep on dead ahead. I made notations of the altitude, motor revolutions per minute, air temperature, oil temperature, and air speed in the log of the ship at 22 o'clock. Although it was pretty dark at sea then, I knew it was just 6 P.M. and broad daylight in New York.

Twenty-three minutes later I got the best position we had all the way across. The moon came up as Wiley hung the ship on the propeller and barged upstairs. We came out at about 9,000 feet and caught up with the sun before it set behind us. We were above the cloud stratum which stretched before us and hid the ocean. Great mounds of cloud bulged menacingly above the mass ahead, so I worked fast while Wiley kept on climbing.

I managed to get a sight at the moon and sun to establish what we call the moon-and-sun line fix. By drawing two circles about these two centers, showing the angle at which they were from us, I could fix our exact location from the point at which the two arcs crossed. It was a good thing I got it, because from there on our work was to be well cut out, but of course I couldn't tell that then.

So, with our position known at 51° N. and 42° W., I began to compute a course on dead reckoning "just in case." At 23:15 I figured the wind out of the west and altered the course to 88°.

It was midnight on the ocean, according to Greenwich time, and we were in the first hours of true night when I got my next sight of the moon, which was now well above the first-quarter segment of the sky ahead. At 00:32 (32 minutes after midnight), we passed position 5 at exactly 53° 15' N. and 35° W. The wind seemed to be turning off to the northwest. I spent the next few minutes holding my drift indicator on a large spot in the cloud below, trying hard to get some guide to our drift. Failing, I decided to alter the course again to 100°, or just south of east. This figure included the current variation of 30° for that area, which made our magnetic course 70°, or about east-northeast.

With this data, Wiley dived down through the clouds carefully for 5,000 feet or more. We were then plunging right through the center of that deep, black bank. There he pulled up and flattened the dive so that we were losing only about 200 feet a minute. The air-speed meter was reading 175 all the way along that shallow dive. With the wind we knew we had on our tail, we must have been making "plenty knots" for the next 15 minutes. Then we came out into the "clear." It seemed that the long drop through the clouds didn't affect Wiley's sense of proportion, for he kept the dials on the instruments almost stationary throughout. It was a great relief to know that he could do it, if only for a quarter of an hour.

By the clear, I meant that we left the clouds above. We could just about see the ocean some 2,000 feet below. It sure was black then, and we had to put out all the lights in order to see anything at all.

That condition did not last long. At 1 o'clock we ran into heavy rain. It grew worse as we went on, until Wiley called back that he was going up again. I felt him adjust the stabilizer, and we commenced a long climb. Almost fearfully I put out the light and watched the luminous dials of the duplicate set of flying instruments I had on my board.

There wasn't any use in looking out because the clouds pressed hard against the windows.

For more than half an hour I sat there with my eyes glued on the fascinating, glowing dials. Once the ship trembled, the air speed took a sudden drop, and the compass swung wide out to the right while the liquid in it bounced around and the card tilted askew. It seemed as if the torque had taken hold of the ship and it was starting to get away from Wiley.

"Hey!" I fairly screamed through the tube. I had heard about dropping out of the clouds in a spin.

"Hey, what?" Wiley's voice came back.

But by that time the indicator had returned to normal again, so I merely said, "Oh, nothing. Just keep on dead ahead."

"Don't bother me with your damn directions now. Wait till we get out of this soup, and then I'll be tickled to death if you can tell us where we are," Wiley answered in his longest speech of the flight up to that time.

Right then and there I made up my mind that back-seat driving had no place in the "Winnie Mae." I turned away from the instruments and tried mental calculations in dead reckoning from our last position. For as much as 10 or 15 seconds I kept my mind off the blind flying.

But it was no use. Those glowing fingers on the instrument board held a fascination for me that was irresistible. The altimeter was showing a steady rise, and when it passed 8,000 feet, I figured we would come out in the open again.

Periodically, I tried to peer from the window. The needle of the altimeter passed 9,000, then 10,000, then 11,000, but still no sign that there was anything in the world but us two and a lot of fog. I know now what it means to be in solitary confinement. I didn't want to bother Wiley. He had his hands as full as they could be. So I just sat, and sat, and then sat some more. I didn't dare move for fear the shifting of my weight might provide him with more bewildering evidence as he tried to tell which wiggles of the ship were due to air currents and which were the navigator's foolishness.

At 1:30—it seemed as though it should have been high noon and that we had been flying blind all that time—I made an entry in the log book:

"Flying blind."

When I looked at my writing, after we had landed, I was afraid somebody who was a handwriting expert might see it and read my mood from it. I didn't change it, though.

At 1:43, by my Greenwich watch, Wiley asked for my guess at our location.

"We ought to be well over halfway," I said. "By my closest figuring we should be near 54° 07' N. and 30° W.; 1,050 miles out from Harbor Grace. We are making better time than on the flight from Roosevelt to there. We've been out only a little over 6¼ hours."

"How far is that from land?" he queried.

"Wait a minute while I figure it out," I answered.

It was a relief to have something to do. I grabbed up the log book in which I had the positions charted with the distances between each of them. The wild mark where I stabbed at position 11, which was just about on the tip of the Irish Coast, still bears mute evidence to my haste, if I can call it that now.

"Roughly, 925 miles," I replied.

"O.K. What kept you?" he answered.

"You figure it out for yourself and don't tell a soul," I bantered. This feeble attempt at levity seemed to ease things, and I resolved that we should have more of it. Wiley's next question dispelled such thought, however, and I returned to business.

"Doc Kimball's weather map shows we ought to get better weather to the south," he said. "How about swinging down a little?"

"Righto," I said. "Make your swing slow, and I'll keep track of the course we follow so we won't get lost. Fly about 150° for half an hour."

He swung, and I pulled down a chart. I drew our regular course in to the point where I thought we should be at that time. Then I plotted the line off to where the 150° steering should bring us in half an hour.

But we didn't seem to get anywhere nearer clear weather so we changed back to our regular 100° at the end of the half hour. I told Wiley to hold that until I figured out how much to alter the course to the north to hit our true track at position 8. After computing a bit, I called to him, "Swing back up to 77° and hold that."

"O.K., and I'll hold this altitude instead of trying to look for breaks," he replied. "Don't worry about the blind flying. The old ship is loaded just right now and almost flies herself. I haven't touched the stick for nearly an hour except to steady it once in a while."

We flew on until 4:25, when suddenly it began to get light. We came out in the early morning and left the clouds piled high to the rear. They billowed out pure white as high as we could see. Far above us was a thin layer of white and below us a thick stratum of darker rain clouds. We couldn't see the water or anything else below.

From the lightness of the cloud layer, far ahead and to the right I could see a spot lighter than the rest. I had to look a long time, but I finally figured out that the sun should be somewhere behind that spot.

I made some hurried calculations and then decided to hold the course farther south.

"We should be near position 8 now, and our chart calls for 105¼° from there, so swing to the right," I said.

That wasn't accurate navigation. It was just an experi-enced guess, but I must have been nearly right, to judge from where we came out.

The clouds piled up ahead again about 2 hours later. It had been quite a respite to be able to see, to know it was daylight, to feel that we were nearing our goal and getting closer by 150 or more miles each hour. I just let my thoughts run. I wondered what Wiley was thinking about.

"What are you thinking about?" I asked through the unsatisfactory tube. It was a poor way to obtain the only companionship I had.

"Nothing," came the answer, and remembering what he had told me of learning to keep his mind alert by prac-ticing thinking nothing at all, made me wonder all the more. How could a man sit and not think? Well, it is still a puzzle to me.

At 6:25, when I figured we ought to be about 100 miles, maybe a little less, from the Irish Coast, we ran plumb into the rain clouds again. It was even more bewildering in the half light than it had been in the pitch blackness of the night. That somber gray of the opaque curtain outside was stifling. I longed to open the door and shout.

But old Wiley just plodded on—if you can call 150 an hour plodding. He held the ship on an even keel and kept to his course. From the immovable indicators on my in-struments the ship might just as well have been on the ground with its tail resting up on a barrel. From time to time I would give him directions.

"A little more to the right." "A little more to the left." Those were the only words I uttered.

He would comply immediately. I was glad not to be a pilot. It would irk me to have to take directions like that. But faith is Wiley's long suit, and it surely does seem to get him places.

On and on we tore a hole through that dense, misty

grayness. We were swallowed up as it closed in behind. No sign of life, no guide to our path.

One degree or more each half hour or so we kept swinging to the south. At last Wiley shouted through the tube, "Do you think we should be over land now?"

I looked at the chart and at my watch. It was nearly 11 A.M. The people in New York were just getting up, at least those who rise between 6:30 and 7 were. I figured what our position should be.

"I don't know exactly how much time we lost on that detour or how much wind we've had on our tail for the past 5 or 6 hours, but if we have been making better than 140 we ought to be over Ireland," I replied.

"Well, hang on. Let's go down and see if this stuff has any bottom," he said.

Now I don't know whether any of you have ever been in that position, or not. Here we were, 'way, 'way up. We could see nothing. We were going down. We might not be able to see anything on the way down. The fog might extend right down to the ground. I thought of that Empire State Building again and remembered how it stuck up through the clouds that day on the way back from Dr. Kimball's office.

Down, down, down, and still down we went for the next 20 minutes. At times we dropped so fast my head filled up, an indication of almost sheer descent. The plane flew steadily, however, if fast, and nothing hit us. The color of the clouds varied from snowy white to deep brown-gray.

"It looks as if these things were breaking up," Wiley called back.

"If you see anything that looks like a hole, duck around and investigate it while we still have some altitude," I replied.

He did just that. A blinding whiteness enveloped the ship. We cut through it and turned back on our tracks. In making his turn, Wiley dropped the nose slightly so that there would be no danger of stalling. It was a sort of diving turn. We had a little trouble locating that white spot but when we did—

"Water!" I shouted through the tube.

It was still about 1,500 feet below us.

"Water—hell! Land!" Wiley said dryly. So ironic was his tone that I felt abashed. He could see in all directions, whereas I could see only down and behind the ship.

But in the continuance of the turn a rugged shore line came into view.

And that is the story of the flight across the Atlantic on one Tuesday night.

7

JUNE 24

FROM CHESTER TO BERLIN

(POST)

ONCE IN MY LIFE BEFORE THE FLIGHT AROUND THE WORLD, I had an experience which I have never forgotten. After my accident at the drilling rig, I thought I might be blind. For several days I was in total darkness in the hospital with bandages over my eyes. When the doctor removed the bandages, one eye reacted to the lights and shadows. Little tremors ran up and down my back. A faith was born within me in that most emotional moment of my life. With a will to see and faith in the doctors, I gradually brought my one eye up to the point where it was superior to the two of the old days.

But even that seemed like a trifling experience compared with the one I had as we dropped through that swirling mass of mist on the morning of June 24, 1931. The windshield before me was wet and frosted with mist. The damp air in the cockpit made my clothes sticky.

Suddenly a shadow, darker than the rest of the world, flitted across the nose of "Winnie Mae." What was it? I brought the stick back and to the left to keep the ship from the steep diving turn.

A glance at the altimeter showed 2,300 feet. Even discounting an abnormal drop in the atmospheric pressure due to local barometric conditions, we should still have had some 1,500 feet of altitude. The ship was resuming normal flight, and we were going back on our course. I hadn't noticed the compass reading when that black specter shifted across the window.

With the motor wide open, I turned again in a wide flat sweep. This time I picked up the shadow on the side and lower than at first. I suppose that was because the ship was nearly level. Keeping the shadow in sight, I circled cautiously. From then on I lost only a few feet each minute. The mist grew thinner, and we flew right along the ceiling, still circling. It was like coming out of a dark tunnel into the light.

There was land!

Just then Harold called through the tube, "Water!" But I, somewhat excitedly, shouted back, "Land!"

A small town was beneath us. I didn't know what it was, but I headed for the open side. The air was still pretty hazy, but in comparison with what we had been through it seemed like bright sunlight. Gosh, it felt good to look at something that didn't wiggle every time you took your eye off it!

In less than 20 minutes I saw an airport. Just a couple of hangars and an open field. Well, we were headed for Berlin, but who cared? I shot over toward the landing field just about as fast as "Winnie" could wind up her propeller. And then I cut the gun, took one look at the wind indicator, glided off leeward, and turned in for a landing.

The first touch of the wheels gave me even more of a thrill than had that dimmed light, years before, which told me I could still see. As we rolled to a stop, three or four men came running across the field. I could see from the uniform trousers they wore that they were army men. I flipped back my visor and pulled myself up so that my head and shoulders stuck out above the roof.

Gatty was already out. My watch said it was 18 minutes to 8. But that couldn't be right. I held my wrist up to my ear to see if the watch were going. It was.

I was in too much of a stupor to think or to talk. The sound of the engine was still in my ears. When I opened my mouth to ask Gatty where we were, I couldn't hear the sound of my own voice.

By this time the officers were running around the tail of the ship. Gatty was trying to tell them something, but I guess he was having the same sort of ear trouble. In a minute I learned that we were in England.

Before that, I had had no idea whether we had picked out Ireland, Scotland, or Wales. All I knew was that we had found land, and any land would have looked good as a place to set down "Winnie Mae."

It was not only England, but the Sealand Airdrome of the Royal Air Force, about 10 or 15 miles from Liverpool. The officers had already had a telegram from a place called Bangor, in Wales, stating that we had been heard upstairs in the clouds. That little town we had passed turned out to be a place called Chester.

Suddenly I began to remember that we had started to go all the way around the world. I asked questions about the weather and listened, almost mechanically, to the reports.

They sure do go out of the way for you on one of those R. A. F. fields. They offered us gas, but we didn't need much as we wanted to keep the ship as light as possible for the flight on to Berlin. They said they would gas the plane according to that desire. I suppose they figured our hourly consumption by the figures on their own planes.

But they wouldn't hear of our leaving without lunch.

Yes, lunch! My 18 minutes to 8 was New York time. It was 11:42 in England. We had some good old English roast beef like that advertised by New York chophouses. Neither the idea of food nor the feeling of hunger had ever entered into the details of our flight across. But I certainly did eat at the Sealand Airdrome!

The fellows from the R. A. F. were so nice that we hated to leave, but naturally we were anxious to get on our way as soon as possible. When they understood that we were trying to make a record trip around the world, they helped us in every way possible to get away in a hurry. Judging from the efficient way they did things, I should say that they certainly must know their business.

There was nothing unusual about our take-off. It was just like hundreds of other "Winnie Mae" take-offs. We were off in 500 feet and climbed fast to the ceiling. I gave Harold a map marked with distances, compass course, and other details, which the fellows at the airdrome had handed me, and he allowed for the deviations in my compass.

We passed north of London, went out over Norwich, and left England behind at Lowestoft, all within 1 hour and 20 minutes. We had stayed at Sealand 1 hour and 20 minutes, and I opened up to make up for the lost time. The haze had burned away, and the weather was getting better every minute as we headed over the North Sea.

The flight over the North Sea was ideal for visibility. We saw an odd boat or two when we swooped down to have a look, and I had to restrain myself from cavorting around in the air in a victory demonstration.

I relaxed a little then, and violated all my rules by reflecting a bit on the past 24 hours. This is the way my mind ran about those hours over the Atlantic.

I had thought that flying across Long Island Sound

would be a sample of ocean flying. Now I knew that flying across Long Island Sound was the same kind of sample of ocean flying as rowing a boat on the pond in Central Park would be of sailing the "Leviathan."

We were hardly out from Harbor Grace when I saw the ocean swell. I figured what kind of landing one might make on that moving floor. Dropping the bottom out of the ship to find that the intended 15 feet of altitude had suddenly become 25 or 50 feet less than nothing would be disconcerting, to say the least. And one wouldn't have time to say any more than the least, either.

The blind flying wasn't as bad as I had expected. All it took was plenty of concentration and alertness so that the plane would never get started off the straight path. I had found the air-speed indicator a great help in checking up on the other instruments. Each variation in the rate-of-climb or bank-and-turn indicators had showed within a fraction of a second on the air speed of the plane.

My thoughts on the way over had been what I had made them. It had not been easy in that blind condition to keep from thinking at all, so I had tried little tricks with the plane. Things like seeing how long it took for the slightest pressure on a rudder pedal to show up on the instruments, or timing the lag on the compass, or trying to hum to the rhythm of the vibration moment of the propeller. (There is always a point of vibration which makes a sort of throb at regular intervals of about a second. This can easily be adjusted to music, even by some one, like myself, who is not a musician at all.) But in no sense did I have to whistle to keep up my courage. I knew what my airplane would do under certain conditions, and I had devoted myself to keeping those conditions constant for ordinary straight flight.

Things had become very tiresome after a while, and my

mind had set in a single track, so that when I landed near Chester, for several minutes I was mentally still flying the plane through fog.

My reflections on the Atlantic crossing were cut short by the sight of land. We picked up the coast of Holland on the very spot marked by our British friends. The Hague was on our right and the outskirts of Amsterdam stood out to the left. We knew we were right by the little indentations of the coast which were pictured by the map. We had been right on the course marked by the British officers when we had left England over Lowestoft, just 9 miles south by east from Yarmouth. From then on I had stuck to the course according to the compass. We didn't even figure any drift. What with the map in good detail, and Harold as weary as he could be, we had just let it go at that, figuring we could pick up our course again at whatever position we came over land. It took us only about 40 minutes to cross the North Sea, and we knew we couldn't get far off the course in that time.

The R. A. F. lads had told us to fly south of the Great Circle to pick up better landmarks and the airway between Amsterdam and Berlin. I could follow the U. S. air-mail routes, so I didn't ask how the European airways were marked. If they are marked at all, I don't know it. It may be easy for pilots on the Amsterdam-Berlin run to find their course as we do at home, by knowing a hill, by recognizing a town, or just by luck, but it was not easy for us. And it seemed silly to Harold to start "shooting the sun" when he had a perfectly good map in front of him.

"Swing to the left," he said. "Hold your course about 97°."

As the "Winnie Mae" swung her nose toward the east, we picked up the Rhine where it flows through The Netherlands. That gave us a landmark on which to start the trip to Berlin. I was very tired then, and had plenty of trouble keeping the course. Most of all, the thickly-settled country bothered me.

If we had been fresh and in trim, I don't suppose the country we flew over that afternoon of June 24th would have bothered us, but tired as we were, we just naturally roamed around a bit. From the canals and quaint houses of Holland we ran into the villages of Westphalia. We were a little south of our course by this time, so we began to check up. About halfway to Berlin, we picked up Hannover and made a landing there to get exact bearings and directions to the Tempelhof airdrome on the outskirts of Berlin. It was an hour's run.

At Hannover we created a little sensation. The airport people were more than obliging. We were so tired that we forgot all about our fuel supply, taking it for granted that the Englishmen had put enough in the tanks for us to make Berlin. But English engines must import their carburetors from Scotland and run on short rations, because when taking off from Hannover at 1.30 by my watch (New York time), we suddenly realized that our gas supply was nearly gone.

We dropped down again. The airport people in Hannover were shocked, I guess, that we showed so little method in our flight. But they gave us gas, and in 45 minutes we hopped off again, headed for Berlin and a rest. We didn't see any of the famous sights on the way, because we were too tired to look. Anyway, the great factories and mills of Germany would have looked like Gary, Indiana, to me, because I just couldn't get up any more enthusiasm than was needed to manage the "Winnie Mae."

I did get a little kick out of the first sight of our goal. I was impressed with the nearness of the airport to the big squares in the town. I guess when that Hohenzollern emperor ordered the imperial engineers to build a good parade ground, so the people would be inspired with the

splendor of the nation, he didn't realize that he was building what would be the best airport of any large city in the
world. Even out in roomy Oklahoma we can't seem to get
the airports so close to town.

And that airport was busy. Nearly every air line in Europe runs at least one plane a day into Tempelhof. From
the different types along the line you could pick out planes
from nearly every nation. There were big Junkers passenger ships, a couple of Bernards from France, Handley
Pages from England, one or two metal ships from Russia,
ships from Poland, Austria, and Italy in those lines. We
added the United States to the list.

I circled carefully, and was wide awake by the time I was
ready to set "Winnie Mae" down for the night. A big crowd
had turned out, and I had to make sure the sky was clear
of other ships before I turned the nose in for the last act of
the flight. The airport was just a little bit short for landing
a ship as fast as the Lockheed, and what with my slowed
reactions from lack of sleep, I didn't want to take any
chances. I got down all right, landing at 8:30 Berlin time
(3:30 in New York).

I had figured we could duck out and get in some of our
lost sleep. We tried it, but the hospitable Germans stopped
us. No rest for the weary was the idea there that day. I
had seen pictures of crowds taking people on their com-
bined shoulders, but that was the first time I was ever
hoisted up so that everybody could look at me. Above the
heads of the mob which surrounded the ship and dragged
us out, I got a glimpse of Harold being rushed away on
the shoulders of a couple of husky German enthusiasts
toward a little observation balcony. I'd have rather flown
another 100 miles or more than have been carried to my
bed that way, but that's what happened to me, anyway.

People began making noises in a language I couldn't
understand. A group of reporters surrounded me and fired

questions at me. But when I only mumbled a few words of English in reply, they soon turned away disgustedly. Harold laughed aloud at my embarrassment. He had been in foreign countries before and knew what to do.

A reporter from a New York paper came over, and was good enough to help us out in answering the questions of the Germans. He translated the requests of the photographers, and in a short time everyone was happy. We would tell him a few details of the flight, and he would translate them to the others. And from the crowd beyond the reporters, loud guttural voices would shout:

"*Hoch!*"

Then the crowd would cheer, and we would have to wait until the noise died down before we could answer any more questions.

A man from a broadcasting company came hurrying over and told us in English that a transatlantic broadcast had been arranged. He handed us a cablegram from New York in which we were instructed to talk over the radio.

That was a job. Neither of us had planned on doing any public speaking, and I guess we both were a little stagestruck. The radio man could talk good English, however, and he helped us out a lot. I was so tired and deaf I could hardly speak, but I mumbled into the microphone he held in front of me:

"Hello, Germany and America!"

Then the announcer asked, "How do you feel after your flight across the ocean?"

Now, under such conditions, what could I say? I simply stammered in my best parlor language:

"Very good, so far, now that the worst is over."

But at that, I outtalked Harold for once. He was put through the same thing.

"I haven't a thing to say," was his reply.

But the announcer wouldn't be satisfied with that.

"It isn't what you say," he whispered. "The folks back home want to hear your voice."

So Harold made one more try.

"I was very glad to have landed in Germany," he said, like a scared kid making a school recitation.

Then the announcer gave up. I guess he thought we were a couple of poor talkers. Maybe he was right.

Next we were greeted by a large group of officials. Men such as Ministerial Director Brandenburg of the National Traffic Ministry, Max Wronsky, director of the Luft Hansa Air Line, who shook our hands most cordially and talked to us in English, and City Councilors Adler and Sauernheimer, who gave us flowers and champagne and guided us through the crowd to the airport restaurant.

During the meal I took our hosts by surprise when I asked for a glass of ice water. There was good port wine in front of me, and all the beer we wanted, and the Germans just couldn't understand that thirsty Americans needed water. The windows around the balcony restaurant were crowded, and I could see the people nudge one another when I started drinking the water.

It seemed as if the cheering would never die down. The newspapermen broke through and came into the room to press us with more questions. By this time there were many English and American reporters present.

Some one in the crowd around shouted in English at the reporters:

"*Donnerwetter!* Let the poor fellows eat."

But we felt we had to answer the questions, because the reporters were so nice about it. Then we went to the police station in the city and had our passports looked at. There was some little trouble about our not having had them visaed by the consul in New York, but the officials let us get away with that.

I had a tough time relating my experiences on the flight

to a representative of the New York newspaper which had bought the story from me. I went to my room in the airport hotel with him and several times he had to prod me when I fell asleep in the middle of a sentence.

Harold went to sleep and we let him rest. At 11 o'clock that night, Berlin time, I, too, went to bed. The call was left for 5 A.M.

That 2½ hours had been the hardest work up to that time. The reception and telling about the trip had taken a lot of my energy. I slept so soundly that it was a tough job for them to get me out next morning.

It was then that I learned we had broken a record for an Atlantic crossing. Alcock and Brown, the first two flyers to make the trip, had held it for 12 years. Their course was about 230 air-line miles shorter than ours, as they landed in Ireland.

The "Winnie Mae" had won a laurel already, and we were only at the end of the first run.

JUNE 25

FROM BERLIN TO MOSCOW

(POST)

WE BREAKFASTED ON THE BALCONY OF THE AIRPORT HOTEL JUST as the light of Thursday, June 25th, pushed through an overcast sky. Tempelhof is equipped with a good meteorological station and weather reports were flowing in over the telegraph machines. Our weather luck—mostly bad—seemed to be sticking by us. All reports coming in from the east showed rain, fog, and low visibility.

We had only a short day's run ahead of us—the 994 miles to Moscow. A return message to a telegram we sent there stated that it was clear at Moscow, with no rain or fog forecast for another 12 hours. That made Harold and me decide to go, regardless of local conditions. We figured that we could fly blind a good part of the way and then pick up a course good enough to lead us into Moscow before dark. We also thought that if we were forced down, we probably could make up the time lost, as the leg was so short.

I was particularly anxious to get off. Things had been going well with the ship, and I knew that sooner or later we would be delayed for some trifling bit of repair or some necessary servicing. The farther on our way we could get before that happened, the better for us.

The ship was gassed and wiped off. A tractor was hooked on the tow rings and "Winnie Mae" was pulled out on the apron of the hangar. Some maps were given us which Harold thought he could use by comparing with a small atlas he had, although they were in many different languages. We tried to pay our bill, or rather I did, for Harold had no money with him, but the Germans wouldn't let us, and I left with my $34 still intact.

Even at that early hour a few people came out to the airport to see us off. We bade good-by to everybody there and piled into the ship. A mechanic spun the prop for me, and I warmed up for 10 or 15 minutes. I took that long to make sure the gas they gave us was right for the plane. The engine didn't knock badly or seem to slow up under the extra heavy strain of running up the propeller with the plane held tight to the ground behind its wheel chocks, so I gave the signal to have the chocks pulled away.

It was 6:35 by Gatty's Greenwich time when we took off. That was 7:35 Berlin time and 2:35 New York daylight. I pulled back the stick and hung the ship on the propeller until we reached the ceiling of 2,000 feet. There we flew right along the base of a dark cloud bank which promised plenty of rain to Berlin within a short time, if I was any judge of weather. The air was muggy in the tightly closed cockpit, and I opened one of the windows on the right side. It was far enough away from me so that I wouldn't be in a draft.

I had a reason for climbing up as high as I could get and still see the ground. I wanted to try out the motor and be sure we could land again in case that Berlin gas began to heat up the motor. I'm pretty hard to convince on strange gasoline, but there was no detonation and the Wasp

seemed to run just as it had run in Oklahoma, where gasoline is made and alleged to be the best.

"Set our course at 73°," was my first instruction from
Gatty.

"Figure it done already," I replied.

I felt fine and was getting ready to go places with the
"Winnie Mae." Down under us was a railroad running
right on our way, so the course was easy to follow. Here
and there the rails would wind around a hill, while we
could cut straight across. The plane was in good flying trim
so that I could fly it on stabilizer and rudder alone.

We came to the wide Oder River and the city of Küstrin.
As I passed over the center of the town, I dipped the wings
to give Harold a time check. He had asked for this in order
to get a start on computing the line of flight by dead reckoning in case we should have to change to blind flying in
a hurry.

The city reminded me of the river towns in the Middle
West, except that it looked a lot older. Big shops and foundries stood along the water front. The little houses were
clustered together differently from those in United States
towns, and the streets seemed to make more turns. The
center of town, where I gave Harold the signal, had a big
square surrounded by ancient stone buildings. I suppose
it is one of the places tourists rave over and get pictures of
to take home to the folks. I wouldn't have minded getting
one, too, if only just to be able to prove to some of my
skeptical friends that I had really flown over Germany.

It is funny how you can fly all the way across Europe
and not notice much of interest to anyone except another
airplane pilot. The speed is too great, and the details which
give the European countries what Harold calls "atmosphere" are not visible from the air.

Soon we picked up what Gatty said was the River Warta.
We followed it at intervals for a long time. I never saw a

river first wide, then narrow, and then wide again as that one is.

"Check up on your watches," said Harold. "We passed over Küstrin at 7:04½ and it is now 7:10 by Greenwich time."

I looked at my wrist watch and found it was 3:10, New York time. I was keeping it New York time all the way so that I could tell just how long we had been out from Roosevelt Field. The clock on the instrument board I set at 8:10 to conform to German time.

An overhanging bit of cloud interrupted me just then, clapping its way through the propeller wash to warn me that the ceiling was falling down on us. I stuck "Winnie Mae" over on her nose to dodge another big mess of black rain cloud, and we dropped to about 1,000 feet before I pulled up in level flight again.

At the end of that drop we came out over a lot of railroads. They seemed to run in all directions. The country reminded me of the New Jersey marshes on a murky day when you creep up on Newark Airport from the southwest. We saw factories set in among the railroads, with the ground between them mostly waste water and slag dumps. The ship was gradually being forced lower and lower, and keeping within sight of the ground gave me many squeamish sensations in the next 15 or 20 miles. I was down at 400 feet by that time and could see only about half a mile ahead. When buildings and stacks loomed up in front, I would pull back pretty fast to get up. Then I would bang right down again as soon as I felt sure that I was over them.

I found out later that none of those stacks extended up as high as 400 feet, but when one is tearing along toward them, they seem higher than they really are.

That bouncing up and down at 150 miles an hour played havoc with Harold. He was sitting so far back in the plane that he had the sensation of being suspended in mid-air.

"Keep a little more to the right," I heard him call through the tube. "We are getting near Landsberg, so pick up the river and follow it until we get past the town."

I quickly swung toward the right. Not that I had to turn so quickly, but the rapid actions of the past few minutes were becoming a habit. Even the aperiodic compass gyrated a trifle from the speed of the turn, and I must have banked a little too flat, because I heard Harold again:

"Watch those turns! You nearly knocked everything off the table. If we break the sextant, we won't be able to get another around here."

The sextant was hanging from a hook near the roof of the fuselage, and I guess it had slapped against the side of the ship.

In bad visibility it is better to slide your turns flat than to take a chance on slipping a little toward the ground. I decided not to try a very steep bank when I picked up the river. I could avoid the slipping by making the turns wide.

As we picked up the Warta again, a big factory loomed up on the north bank, right in our path.

"Which way?" I called back over my shoulder to Harold.

"Left," came the answer. "And for goodness' sake, take it easy. Things are jumping around back here like dice in a box."

I had to grin at that. But I did swing a little east, and the turn was slower. It was so slow, in fact, that we passed within shouting distance of the factory stack.

I climbed a little as we came out over the river. I didn't want to run into any bridges. I nearly ran into the Hudson River Bear Mountain Bridge once, and I have been a little "bridge shy" ever since.

"Shall I keep on over the river and make the bends with it?" I called back.

"O.K., but watch out for another branch coming in from the right," was the reply.

I moved over above the left bank. It led us along over more marshes, but no factories. Then we came to a big body of water. It looked like a lake, but was really the widening of the river to a big shallow pool in among the marshes.

We got a little relief from the low visibility about this time, but not for long. I climbed up to about 1,500 only to start down again. Up ahead it looked pretty black.

"See if you can raise somebody on that radio and try for a weather report," I suggested to Harold.

I never stopped to think that even if he did get tuned in, few people along our route would understand English, and the request might be taken for a distress signal.

Harold tried the radio, but gave up when, after half an hour of barging across open country, we saw Schneide-mühl appear. In that half light the town might have been Rahway, New Jersey, it was so filled with foundries and mills. Later I learned that a lot of bone dust for filters is made there.

"In a few minutes, we'll cross the border into Poland," my navigator said. "Keep a little to the right. We are allowing a bit too much drift for that north wind. Or else it's turning into a nor'easter. If it is, it will bring down a lot of rain."

Schneidemühl had hardly dropped off our tail when Harold reported that we were on the German-Polish border. As we left the town, we saw the junction of two railroads. A small stream seemed to mark the boundary line where we crossed.

The appearance of the country didn't change, though, except that the occasional farm buildings seemed to be painted better. That section of Poland was formerly a part of Germany, and on the maps all its names are still in German. At 9:30, two hours out from Berlin, we picked up Swiecie. There it began to pour. We were right on the course, and Gatty was getting accurate information on our speed and drift through his gadget which pointed down.

That was the only direction we could see—down, and not more than 300 or 400 feet at that. It was raining so hard that the cattle were huddled in little bunches. They didn't even scatter when the noise of the motor made them bobble around.

Just beyond Swiecie we tore across the Vistula River. It is very wide and runs northeast. It was heavy with barge traffic, and from the smoke of towboats—they didn't look like our tugs—we got the wind direction at north-northeast. All along the shore line of the east bank of the river we saw the best-looking country we had seen in Europe. From the fleeting glance I had of them the crops looked good. I noticed that tractors and high-speed machines were being used for most of the farming. The workers stopped for a moment to stare at the plane as we skipped along through the rain. Evidently those Polish farmers have a different system from ours. When I was a kid, we usually stopped outside work on such rainy days and spent our time fixing harness or machinery indoors.

Then we crossed another border and began a lightning-like flight across East Prussia. Plenty of lakes and smooth fields slipped under the wheels. With an amphibian we could have landed anywhere, even with our few hundred feet of altitude and a dead engine. But the Wasp out front didn't show any signs of weakening.

At Allenstein we picked up a railroad. A train on it was going our way. The freight cars looked strange to me as I recalled the long snakelike overland freights of the Pennsylvania. The smoke from the engine stack drifted off to the right, and we knew that the wind was holding in the same direction.

"Somewhere up this section is where the German war ace, Richthofen, came from," Gatty called.

That impressed me, for underneath the plane, beautiful estates with old stone castles and splendid outbuildings were flicking by. The country was like the Long Island north shore where the captains of American industry spend week-ends. It was hard to realize that the German ace came from so luxurious a setting.

But even the beauty of Central East Prussia didn't last long with "Winnie Mae" under way. The rain continued, and air currents developed among the low-rolling clouds that made "Winnie" heave first to the right wing tip and then to the left, with a sort of rocking motion. I held the stick rigid and rocked in the opposite direction, but we were so close to the ground that I had to be constantly alert.

In less time than it takes to tell it, we shot across Rastenburg and a cluster of big lakes. Then we thundered across the border again into the eastern section of Poland. Two hours of flying over cattle ranges and farms, and at 12:24 by the clock on the instrument board we crossed low over the boundary of the Union of Socialistic Soviet Republics.

"Well, here we are," came through from Harold.

"Yes," I answered. "Just like the guy falling out the twenty-fourth story window and yelling as he passed the third, 'Well, I'm all right so far.' "

The topography of old Russia is like that of Poland, but the scenery is very different. That crossing of the border line into what is called the greatest experiment in Europe was by far the most pronounced contrast we saw in the entire trip around the world.

We had our first glimpse of the famous Five-Year Plan and its effect on farms. As one born and raised on a farm, I was so interested in the great collective farms that Harold had to repeat his directions to me.

"A little to the right," he would say.

And when I would swing 7° or 8° right, it hardly seemed a minute before he would counter, "Now, a little to the left."

We must have made a nice zigzag track over those farms. They weren't really farms as we know them. Even the big wheat fields of our own West were eclipsed by those flat plains.

In spite of our high rate of speed, we could see the great contrast between the quiet little domains of the Polish farmers, with their small homesteads and neat, but aged, clusters of outbuildings, and the huge, rambling community centers of collective farming. Long barrack-like workers' houses and quantities of modern farm machinery were evidence of a wholesale production scheme.

"How much more to go?" I asked.

"We had 375 miles to go when we crossed the line, and we've been in Russia 29 minutes," Harold replied. "That leaves about 325 miles to go. We're making only about 100 ground speed now. That's some tough wind."

It was just that, and it brought with it the worst weather we had yet encountered.

Five minutes later, 1 o'clock on the dash, it hit us! "It" was a rainstorm like a Kansas cloudburst. I have never seen rain run so thick on a flying airplane. Usually it appears as a lot of little beads of water being blown along by the slipstream. Unless you look for them, you can hardly tell it is raining, except for the way the vision is dimmed.

But that storm which burst right on the nose of "Winnie Mae" as we crossed the West Dvina River left no doubt that it was raining. It actually streamed along the cowling in front of me, and I could see clouds of steam coming out from under the ring around the engine, where the torrent was bouncing off the hot exhaust pipes. It was just as if a fire hose were being turned through that opening in the front of the engine cowl. I was glad that our spark plugs were shielded and the magnetos well behind the heated cylinders.

Worse than all else, I couldn't see. Not seeing here was much worse than it was over the ocean. There we had plenty of altitude and nothing to hit, but hedge-hopping through Russia with about 200 yards' visibility and 100 or more miles an hour speed is enough to make your hair stand on end every time you cross a fence.

That was one of the spots where I appreciated Harold's technique in cross-country work when the visibility is bad. He kept driving me to the left of the course until I began to get a little worried. But that is an old trick of navigators. They deliberately make an error on the way so that when the proper time comes and they know the goal should be reached, the alternate way to turn is evident. If all the errors are on the same side, the goal must be on the other side. Gatty kept to the left on that flight to Moscow because the drift was to the right. Knowing how much drift there was, he could easily steer me more into the wind. That slowed down our speed a little, but it also limited the drift each hour.

So at the next town, a rambling village called Velizh, he called:

"Swing 10 more points to the left."

"We are too far north now," I answered.

"I know that, but we can always turn south, and I want to be sure on which side to find Moscow when we get that far."

We went on that way for some time. I was glad my navigator wasn't one of those fellows who is so certain that he is directly on the course that he gets bewildered when he finds that some change in the wind or something has driven him off.

In a little while Harold said that if we steered a bit to the right, we might pick up another village. I couldn't see anything, and I didn't like the idea of finding houses mixed up in the propeller, but I eased off a little on the pressure I was keeping on the left rudder.

Sure enough, we came through a little clearer weather and the town of Sychevka (try the name yourself!). Being certain of our location, after that hour or more of guesswork, was just like coming in out of the rain. From that town (Harold spelled its name out slowly to me through the tube), it was plain sailing. The rain was getting lighter and the sky clearer.

Still keeping a shade to the left of what we figured was our precise course, we saw Moscow break the flat horizon. We knew when we were getting near, for we could see the railroad converging. We ran along until we were almost even with the city on our right, and then, with a triumphant gesture, I banked around and headed southeast to circle the city before we landed. It was still early, so we tore around the old city twice to have a look at it. We saw the old buildings and squares, the crooked, cobbled streets, and the newer outskirts built up since the Soviet regime.

We saw two airports and had a little trouble telling which was which. We had been told to land on the commercial field, since the other was a military post on which strangers from capitalistic lands were forbidden to land. There was no crowd to mark the one on which we were expected, but an automobile, scurrying across the runway on the field to the left, gave us the impression that that was our field. When I flew over the other field to get into the wind for the glide down, I had a check on that, as I saw on the line some Junkers metal planes rigged up as bombers.

We ran in a little high over the fence, slipped into the left, and set "Winnie Mae" down. We were tired from our long fight with the elements.

Our arrival was the least spectacular thus far on our trip. There were only about two dozen people on the airport. They included the airport personnel, American newspapermen, and a few representatives of Soviet societies. We were taken in tow by the members of *Ossoaviakhim* (Society for Aviation and Chemical Defense) and the *Voks* (Society for Cultural Relations with Foreign Countries). They escorted us to the office of the commandant of the field. The flying field was just like a well-regulated military post. Our reception was frigidly formal and efficient.

Our passports and papers were looked over by the authorities, and we left orders for fueling and servicing the ship. Most of the equipment on the airport was either German or of German design and Soviet manufacture. We were surprised to be taken into the city in a nice shiny American automobile.

The Savoy Hotel was better than we had anticipated, and the sight of a comfortable bed was too much of a temptation for me. I flopped right on it, clothes and all, and had to be forced to clean up for a formal nine-course dinner which had been arranged by *Ossoaviakhim*. That organization was the most cordial to us of any we met in Russia, and without its coöperation our work of flying on would have been much harder.

The dinner lasted until after 11 o'clock and as we had landed at 5:40 (10:40 A.M. in New York), it is not hard to imagine how tired we were. The dawn comes in Moscow, or "Moskva," as the Soviets call it, at 2 A.M., so we left a 1 o'clock call, which gave us only 2 hours to sleep.

Only 3 days had passed; we were nearly halfway around the world and ahead of schedule. Those were my happy thoughts as I dropped off to sleep the moment I hit that comfortable bed.

9

JUNE 26

FROM MOSCOW TO NOVO-SIBIRSK

(GATTY)

THE DEADLY SENTENCE, *V-KATORGU*, WHICH USED TO BE pronounced on prisoners dooming them to a life of hard labor in Siberia, seemed mild compared to the call which got us out of bed in Moscow, just two hours after we had left the dining room. But I shook Wiley, and within a few moments we were on our way to breakfast. We paid little attention to the food placed before us. In fact, we were still only half awake when, at 1:45 A.M., we emerged from the hotel in charge of the solicitous *Ossoaviakhim* representatives.

It was already getting light. The gray dawn gave promise of good weather, and the wind had shifted around to the northwest. We had a long way to go and little information to go on, but the promise of help from the wind cheered us, and by the time the shiny car reached the flying field, we felt ready to get under way again.

Somehow, by the time we arrived in Moscow, I had begun to grow attached to the "Winnie Mae," and it was like finding a lost friend to recognize her at the airport that morning. Up to that time, the white Lockheed had been "just another airplane" to me, but in that gray dawn I understood Wiley's change of mood whenever he approached that ship.

The advance information I had brought along for the next leg of the flight was pretty sketchy, and I was overjoyed at a set of maps that the *Ossoaviakhim* men gave me. All my material had consisted of plotted observation marks set out on an old map of pre-revolutionary Russia. Instead of picking up landmark checks on the course, I had intended to navigate just as I had done on the Atlantic flight. These new maps would make the flight less tiring and more interesting as I watched for cities and mountains en route. For Wiley, of course, the work was to be the same. He would still sit with his eyes on whatever horizon he could get, either the artificial one on the board or the actual wavy one of the Urals.

We were all set to go when we discovered that a grave error had been made in fueling the ship. Poor old "Winnie Mae's" tanks had been filled nigh to bursting, making her weigh heavily on the landing gear.

Wiley swore softly as he admitted his fault to our host from *Ossoaviakhim*. He had not been explicit enough about our gallon unit of measurement, and the airport mechanics had loaded the plane with imperial gallons—277 cubic inches as compared with the U. S. Gallon of 231. We had nearly as much on board as we had had on the take-off from Harbor Grace. Wiley felt that we couldn't get that much of a load off on the Moskva runway.

There was nothing to do but take some gas out. We wanted to bleed it out through the line at the bottom of the tank, but the airport officials feared the fire hazard if so much fuel were dumped on the ground, so they started a syphon going.

The precious minutes wore on. We knew that if we

didn't get away quickly, we would have to finish the flight in darkness, as we had 2,600 miles, or about 17 hours, 20 minutes at 150 miles an hour, to go.

Time after time the mechanics lost the suction on the syphon. Then they spent more time sucking on the end of the small hose. Still muttering, Wiley watched them, admonishing the workers in no uncertain tones. Of course, they couldn't understand a word he said, but two or three times the young woman who was acting as interpreter blushed and changed her translations a little.

At last, with that spirit of energetic self-confidence which characterized the take-off preparations at Harbor Grace, Wiley called to me, and we started doing the job ourselves.

While we were keeping the mechanics busy placing empty cans under the hose outlet, the pretty young interpreter was kept busy translating a steady barrage of information and instructions issued by a Russian representative of the Amtorg Trading Corporation in New York. We learned that the fuel was of good quality and that we could get more of the same grade all the way along the line to Khabarovsk, 3,918 miles away.

To the warnings in regard to flying over the Urals, Wiley said, "Shucks! After that flight over the ocean, the Urals will be duck soup to us." And the white-skirted, red-bereted young interpreter announced his boast with much accompanying excitement.

She was a particularly bright young woman, a graduate of Hunter College in New York City, and the wife of an engineer doing work in Russia. She quickly analyzed our possible difficulties after leaving Moskva, and worded twenty telegrams for us, addressed to all of the various airports along the route where we might have to land with the coming of darkness. Then, on telegraph blanks, she wrote out instructions that we might take with us to the airport commandants. They were so worded that by merely filling in blank spaces with time figures, we could report our landing and take-off times en route. She prepared another set of telegraph sheets, leaving blanks for the number of gallons of fuel—and she made explicit the kind of gallons. Truly, a remarkably efficient young woman!

Wiley champed and fretted. The calmness he exhibited in the air was absent as soon as the propeller of the "Winnie Mae" stopped turning. As the clock on the administration building of the airport passed 3 o'clock, 4, and finally 4:30, local time, he began to get so excited that I was afraid he would be all worn out before we got started.

But at 4:35 in the broad sunlight of a beautiful morning, Wiley climbed into his spacious chair behind the control column. I fastened the boot on the propeller tip after the mechanics had primed the cylinders with a few turns of the blades. They helped me pull the rope attached to the boot as Wiley turned the switch on and spun the booster magneto by hand.

The Wasp "caught" on the first pull, and roared loudly. The staccato notes of the exhausts dispelled all of Wiley's impetuous mood. The last of his fretting was blown back by the propeller wash, it seemed, and he was once more the efficient and tranquil pilot, businesslike and patient.

"Let's go, kid," he shouted above the swish of the idling air screw.

After many hasty good-bys, I climbed in, and we taxied down the field almost at flying speed. The tail bumped along, and everything in the cabin danced about. I hung on as my loose chair slid backward, and I clung to my instruments for their dear lives, and maybe our own; for we had a lot of navigating to do yet before the familiar ground of Roosevelt Field would appear.

The Soviet authorities and pilots had advised us to stop

at Krasnoyarsk for fuel, but between ourselves we agreed that Novo-Sibirsk would be a better place to refuel. It fitted in with the daylight period of the day's run as it was 310 miles nearer Moskva than Krasnoyarsk, which was within 428 miles of our goal at Irkutsk.

That was what we talked about as I stuttered and pitched around in that hectic ride down the runway. I hit my mouth on the transmitter, and possibly I said a few things that would have made our little interpreter run for cover and ear muffs.

But to judge by the way Wiley wheeled around into the wind, he evidently didn't think that the taxi ride was fast at all. He must have given the rudder a savage kick, for I heard it slap against the stop as he gave the throttle a jab to blow the tail around. The left wheel skidded on the inside of the turn as he jammed the brake, and "Winnie Mae" pirouetted and pointed her nose to the northwest, into the wind.

And was that field bumpy? Well, two or three times on that run of less than 300 yards, before we bounced into the air, I fully expected the struts on the landing gear to come up through the cabin. We were first on one wheel, then on the other. Wiley had his hands full keeping the thing straight at our 70-mile speed.

Then off we went. The last I remember of Moskva was the little gathering of hospitable people standing on the apron of the hangar, waving, as we roared overhead with full throttle in a climbing turn.

We didn't waste any time flying up-wind to get altitude. Wiley stuck his right wing down, and we swung around quickly to the course—78° magnetic. And then we started "going to town." Relentlessly Wiley "poured the soup" to that engine. Like a frightened colt, "Winnie Mae" increased her usual steady lope to a wild gallop, as she ripped a hole through the Soviet air (I understand that the communistic properties run in three dimensions), and things started slipping by those windows so fast that I had to hurry to keep up with the map.

The first entry in the log that day read:

"2:01 G., took off from Moscow, s/c 78½° (M), for Kazan."

The hasty script of the log book is mute evidence of the speed at which we traveled that morning. Within a few minutes we left the railroad we were supposed to follow for 20 miles, and it was lost in its long sweep to the right across the plains. The collective farm areas still predominated, and on this fine morning the workers were already busy keeping up with the machines in the fields. They could hardly take time to stop and watch us as we thundered along.

Strangely enough, my first sight for drift revealed that we were sliding about 3° to the left. That showed a south wind. I must have changed just after we had taken off.

"Watch for smoke and see if you can get a good check on the wind direction," I called to Wiley. "We sure are 'going to town.' "

"Wind looks from the southwest," he called back. "I caught it on that steam tractor back there. And did you see how many of those operators of heavy machinery were women?"

"Thanks for the first remark. I am too busy keeping up with this map to bother about the other one," I replied. "I wish this wind would be more from the west and less from the south. It would help make up for those 3 hours we lost."

An hour and twenty minutes out of Moscow, we crossed the Oka River, and its course paralleled ours some distance to the left. A quick check on the ground speed surprised me. We were making only 152 miles an hour. I guess the impression I had during the first 5 minutes that the speed was so great had been due to the shifting wind passing through the west quarter and blowing for a few minutes straight on the tail.

Eight minutes past the Oka, we ran along over the famous Volga. That boatman song is all wrong. They have tractors to pull the boats upstream, at least in the part of the river near Moskva. We followed the river to Vasil, and unless I missed them when I took time out from sightseeing to get two checks on the course and drift, and relayed instructions to veer to 83° and again to 97° on the compass, there wasn't a single boat being pulled by manpower in all that distance. It was thrilling to look at that river, which, if it could speak, could tell so many adventurous tales.

From the drift indicator I figured the wind almost due south, and with a velocity of about 29 miles an hour at our 3,000-foot altitude.

It hardly seemed any time at all before we droned across Kazan, but my Greenwich chronometer showed 4:52, and we had been out 2 hours, 51 minutes. Further proof that we had made better time in the first few minutes of the hop showed on that check, because Kazan was only 320 miles from our starting point. Our ground speed seemed to be slowing up.

Crabbing into the wind with the air speed at 145, we dropped a little lower, to about 2,200 feet, where we found the wind less stiff. At 6:03 (2:03 A.M. by Wiley's New York wrist watch), we crossed Sarapul, in the foothills of the Urals.

A little farther on, Wiley pulled the "Winnie Mae" back on her tail as the mountains appeared on the eastern horizon. The great barrier, which I had been taught formed the protective wall of Moscow and the czarist capital of old St. Petersburg, was a disappointment to me. The Urals in that section are only little hills compared to what I expected to find.

"If they call these mountains, we ought to take them for a ride over the Boeing Line in the Rockies," Wiley said, as we crossed what seemed to be the highest peak.

Our altimeter read only 4,500 feet, and we had a good 2,000-foot clearance. I began to develop a sort of indifference to this prize range of so-called mountains which were supposed to be protective. They certainly didn't give Wiley or "Winnie Mae" any trouble. But Wiley brought me out of my nonchalance with a snap.

He has the same trait that most transport pilots, not flying regular passengers, have. In running out of the wing tanks, he waits until the last minute before he switches to the full tank. He has a little valve running four ways at his feet, and by giving it a quarter turn he can run out of the left wing tank, the right wing tank, the tank over his head in the center section, or from all three at once. He has another valve for the reserve tank of 20-minutes' fuel. But, as I said, he has a trait. He gets the last drop through the line from the running tank by waiting for the motor to starve and quit before he shifts the valve.

Just as I was belittling the Urals to him through the tube, he said, "Pretty bad sittin'-down country, though. Looks like you couldn't set a glider down there without cracking up."

And I had to admit that those trees and rocky cliffs did look forbidding when you thought of being forced down.

Then it came. Blurp—glub—blurp-blup-blup!

Little shivers ran up and down my spine. The ship veered quickly to the right as Wiley stooped for the valve and kicked the rudder inadvertently. For a moment I thought he was swinging to look for a place to land. But he was quick on the trigger, and after a couple more feeble coughs the engine picked up with a roar again, and Wiley straightened out on the 70° course.

He had done that many times before, and there was

really no reason for any apprehension. Coming as it did, however, just after he had called my attention to the bad landing qualities of that puny mountain range, I had been panicky. I had half known that he would catch the engine again before it stopped, but, just the same, I would rather have those running-dry moments anticipated.

"Hey," I called, "the next time your tank is running low, let me know in advance, will you, so I can catch my breath."

But all I got for my pains was a dry laugh, and I rather think he enjoyed the whole affair. Almost every pilot I know does that trick with passengers who are used to flying and who do not pay fare, but the air lines forbid it and reprimand pilots who come in with any tank on the plane totally dry.

We turned a little to the south, coming over the last range of the mountains, and dropped down the east slope over Chelyabinsk, a junction between the railroad from Leningrad and the Trans-Siberian line from Moskva. This town is supposed to have a population of more than 70,000, but they must live in pretty close quarters because the city, sitting up there in the hills, looked so small.

We followed the main line of the railroad for a little while, picking it up off the right wheel and losing it off to the right at intervals for the next 3 hours. At 9:04 we crossed the River Tobol just north of a city called Kurgan (the names are easier to pronounce in western Siberia, though I haven't found out why), where we altered the course from the 90° which led us southeast out of Chelyabinsk to 79°. That pointed "Winnie Mae's" propeller track straight at Omsk, the largest town on the line to Novo-Sibirsk, according to the map I was using.

During this time I had noticed one peculiar thing. The railroad never went closer to the cities than three, four, or—and this was usual—five or more miles. I understand that the road originally was built as a strategic method of troop transport in the campaign for the czar's protection against Japan, and I suppose that the wide berth it gave the towns was designed to speed up its service in its original use. The newer community houses, in which the collective farmers live, are built near the line, but they are few and far between in this area, as the land is scrubby and not very productive. We saw many grazing cattle and creatures which looked to us like black sheep or goats.

I located our position at 55° 30' N. and 70° E. from Greenwich and found that the maps had been leading us quite a little south of our originally planned course. I resolved to keep to the left of the track marked by the men from *Ossoaviakhim* and told Wiley to swing north-northeast until he picked up the railroad which would lead him into Omsk. Our map must have been wrong. I don't know yet on what method of projection it was drawn. It looked like gnomonic, was figured like a mercator, but was as distorted as a polyconic. I had already discovered that the various altitudes, as shown by graded shades of brown, were hopelessly inaccurate.

"These Russian maps are all haywire," I called.

"I guess it's your Russian that's a little rusty. I didn't think much of your conversational ability on the street in Moscow," he answered.

Quite a jokesmith Wiley was turning out to be, although nobody would ever have suspected it!

But, anyhow, as long as I knew the map was in error, I wasn't afraid to use it. It was some guide to the terrain, and I could pick things out in passing by the "hunt" method.

We ripped off a few more miles and then the gleaming rails and the freights of the railroad came in sight. Wiley turned and flashed past the crawling trains as if they were standing still. We still had that southwest wind and were making very good time again.

The wind must have blasted us right along, for it was just 11 o'clock by my official time as we boomed across Omsk. By quick calculations I figured our mileage at 1,588, which showed an average speed of better than 176 miles an hour. That is fast stepping over so long a run, even for "Winnie Mae."

But was I hungry! I recalled a little conference we had had in Moskva, after which we were forced to decline a nice basket of food prepared for us by some kindly soul with human emotions. Had it not been so far back, I would have suggested to Wiley that we return for it. I could just imagine his reply out there in the plains, where he was hurrying that ship like a white streak across the Siberian steppes, trying to get us through to Irkutsk.

"We are making fast time—better than 176 so far," I said nobly, instead of complaining about the inner man. "If the wind holds out, we ought to be in Novo-Sibirsk early. What do you say to a short rest and a start with the sun for our regular schedule at Khabarovsk tomorrow night?"

"O.K. with me," he replied, "but how about the lights for the landing?"

"Well, let's figure it out when we land. I can't figure on an empty stomach," I bargained.

Our speed was so consistently good that we dropped in at Novo-Sibirsk a full hour and a half before we were expected. That was at 13:32 Greenwich, 6:32 local, and 9:32 A.M. New York daylight, according to the three timepieces we were using.

It is sometimes hard for non-navigators to realize that it can be 6:32 P.M. in Siberia and lunch time (1:32 P.M.) in London, when New Yorkers are just getting through their morning mail at 9:32 A.M., and that on all these hours of the same day, the next day is already 1 hour, 32 minutes old at the 180th meridian, known as the International Date Line.

Novo-Sibirsk is a comparatively new city, but already it has more than 121,000 inhabitants, according to the census. It was built originally by the workers who put the railroad through to Manchuria. At this point they had to erect a nine-span bridge across the wide River Ob which flows just west of the oldest part of the city.

With the aid of the blank forms of Russian instructions the young woman interpreter had given us at Moskva, we made arrangements to have the ship gassed. It was nearly an hour before we were satisfied that the plane would be ready to jump again at dawn, which is just after midnight in that part of the world in June.

At the appointed hour, 8 o'clock, the local officials of *Ossoaviakhim* appeared with a Ford automobile, and we had a ride to town in an old-style "Lizzie" over one of the roughest 4 miles of highway I have ever seen. I have heard that you can time the jolts of the rear seat in an Irish jaunting car, and that it is like learning to ride horseback, but no rider on earth could have timed the bumps on that ride from the airport to the city of Novo-Sibirsk.

Once in the town, we were royally greeted by the populace. We were rushed through the passport formalities at the Police Department, and a harassed interpreter, a woman again, plied us with questions and made regular orations to the crowds which followed us through the narrow street to the ancient hotel.

Evidently they had never even heard of a lift there, and our rooms were on the fifth floor. So Wiley and I figured out what our best angle of climb was—it was quite poor— and trudged up the somber staircase. Hot, or even running water, was one of the unknown mysteries in that hotel, too, but we did get a chance to sponge ourselves in the public bath, where the water dropped from a big tank into a tin basin with a slow, maddening trickle. We were just ready to snatch some sleep when our host invaded our sanctum—two hard beds with blankets and no linen—and almost forcibly escorted us to the head of the stairs. It seemed that we had another banquet coming.

Though I had had a bit of black bread and a glass of wine as soon as we had landed, I was still hungry. But Wiley was more in favor of sleep than food, and I had to coax him to attend.

After a perfect landing on the ground floor, we were taken in charge by the official party. There was no dining room in the hotel, so we trekked through the streets to a restaurant, attracting great crowds at our heels and to the blackened windows of the old stone houses.

But the meal was worth it. If you are ever really hungry, go to Novo-Sibirsk. I don't know what kind of steak we had, nor do I know what culinary institution turned out the chef, but for steak it was about the acme of perfection. Even Wiley began to take some interest in the banquet. The hours sped by without waiting for us, and it was 10 o'clock before we realized it. When we explained to the buxom woman who was interpreting that we had only about 3 hours for sleep before a 20-hour flight to Khabarovsk, she hurried us out.

I guess she was pretty tired, too. She was a professional interpreter who had just returned from Leningrad, where she had been working among the engineering sections of American and Soviet development companies. She was much in demand, as she spoke French and German as well as her own language. She said she had been educated in Berlin and that she had never been so busy as now, when she was interpreting for the Russians.

So "home and to bed," with apologies to Pepys. But the 3 hours! I don't see how Wiley dropped off so fast. He just slumped in his clothes on the stone-like platform they called a bed, yanked the blanket up to his chin, and was "out" in a jiffy.

I got in a little Siberian hunting. I worked like a beaver trying to arrange that blanket so that it would be a mattress instead of a cover, as the night was a little close. At last I dropped into a doze. A great man once said, "It's the little things that count," and they did. An hour later I awakened and discovered numerous welts on my face. With a pencil flash light I started on my hunt. And for 2 hours I stalked the foe. Acting as my own beater, pointer, and shot, I had a perfect average. But I was glad to leave the fruitful game preserve.

Wiley slept on, through that dramatic episode of our flight around the world, as serenely as though he were part of the "built for sleep" advertisements of our American magazines.

10

JUNE 27

NOVO-SIBIRSK TO BLAGOVESHCHENSK

(POST)

THE FIRST THING I HEARD SATURDAY MORNING WAS THE MAID banging on the door and yelling something in Russian at the top of her voice. The day was one hour gone, and I wished that we could get that hour back.

Harold was already up. When I heard his tale of woe, it gave me the second laugh on him within a short 24 hours. The first had been when I had got him to admit that he was off the course. This Russian country was sure his oyster, but he couldn't get it open.

The big dinner I had eaten the night before made me so sleepy that I had trouble staying awake, even with the effort of going down that long stairway. I was "flying blind" all the way down and nearly "spun in" on the last step above the second floor. I banged my ankle against the corner of the newel post in that dark hallway, and it hurt me for two days. But I was afraid to tell Gatty, because I was two laughs ahead, and I didn't want to give him anything to score on.

Breakfast was out of the question. It was 1 A.M. and there

are no all-night restaurants in Novo-Sibirsk. We didn't have any luggage, so nothing stood in the way of our making a hasty exit from the hotel.

The ride out to the field in that antique flivver, bumping on every third bump and flying out of control the rest of the time, was no smoother than it had been going in. I thought it should be, because I had had 3 hours' sleep. As a matter of fact, though, the bed had been a bit like a concrete runway, and it had left several sensitive spots on the small of my back.

But we had to keep merry, so on the way out, while Gatty was still boasting of his prowess as a huntsman, I suggested that he run back and leave one of Dr. Suess' Flit drawings with the manager. He didn't see the joke and mumbled something about a "pilot's intelligence." That put another mark on my side of the laugh score, according to my figuring.

The night before, by a system of sign language mixed with garbled French, Harold had specified just how much gas we wanted. We had watched it loaded, or most of it, while we were waiting for the reception car which was to take us into town.

Now, as we came rattling through the gate back to the field, we saw men wheeling out the ship. It didn't take long for us to check her over, and just as it was growing light enough to see the end of the runway, I started the mill. It seemed as if that motor made more noise out there in the middle of Siberia than it or any other motor had ever made before. It was so loud I began to think that I must be getting back the hearing in my bad ear!

"Do you think you can find the course today, son?" I said to Harold, who was practically asleep on his feet.

"No. You take the sextant and the back seat, and I'll fly the ship," he answered.

I lost one on that scrimmage, so I decided to let the

engine drown out his chuckle. He knew that a jig-saw puzzle would mean more to me than that gadget with which he looks at the sun.

The next time I looked around for him he was already inside. I stuck my head over the top of the cockpit and yelled, "Let's go!"

It was a shock to me to hear him answer through the tube:

"Set your course at 71°, Mr. Post, but don't let me hurry you. After all, we still have a lot of time to beat that record."

That runway was just about as smooth as the road we had come from town on, but "Winnie Mae" went faster than the flivver and rode harder along the ground. I didn't even try to pick out the smoothest part of the field. I kicked the ship around by the west fence and fed the old Wasp its breakfast in the form of full throttle. That half ton of iron must have had an appetizer from the way the Wasp took it. "Winnie Mae" started off in a hurry.

I was still laughing as we jolted along for the first 100 yards, but the bumpy run made me work my feet on the rudder too fast for me to stay laughing long. The motor was winding up at 2,200 revolutions a minute as we cleared the hangar, and we were "going places."

Then I settled back. The armchair was so comfortable that I wished I hadn't bothered with a banquet and the hard bed. I figured I could have had about four hours' more sleep if I had used that chair.

We ripped the air wide open across that railhead at Novo-Sibirsk, and in just a few minutes there was nothing in the world to me but good old "Winnie Mae" with her trusty motor, Harold, and a few scrubby fields. I held the compass at 71° and climbed on the way until we were up about 4,000 feet.

I didn't want to go any higher than that because of a

heavy ground haze, which would give Harold trouble in following the map. There were a few clouds out in front that looked like rain clouds, but they were higher up than we were.

"Better pull that course back to 69°," was Harold's first official speech of the day. Joking time had passed, and we were now on serious business. It was not so easy to find a course for 2,300 miles through strange country, and I was sympathetic. For my part, all I had to do was to steer, and I was used to that. "Winnie Mae" steered just the same in Siberia as she did in Oklahoma.

In less than an hour we caught up with the rain clouds, but they weren't bad. Only light rains fell. We didn't even have to drop our altitude in order to see the ground.

We decided, or rather Harold did, to follow the railroad, and only cut the corners. There were plenty of mountains on the direct line between Novo-Sibirsk and Irkutsk, and the weather reports were scant in that section. The country between the railroad and the southern boundary is rather barren and deserted, and we knew that if we were chased down out of the air, we might have trouble getting back to even Siberian civilization.

The country grew rugged and the forests thick. We had been out an hour and a half, and it was then 6:15 local time and 23:15 by Harold's Greenwich chronometer. The dash clock, which I had reset at the last stop, was in tune with the local time, and by the 7:15 on my trusty wrist watch I knew it was dinner time in New York.

For the benefit of those who followed the reports of our trip, I am going to quote New York daylight time after this in my part of the story of the flight. The P.M.'s will be A.M.'s between Siberia and Alaska, and vice versa.

At 7:24 P.M. we passed over Lake Sharipur, which is about 20 miles south from the railroad which makes a wide arc from Novo-Sibirsk to Irkutsk. The road cuts through

Smithsonian Institution Photo No. A332.

Looking none the worse for wear, Wiley Post, *left,* and Harold Gatty, *right,* stand in front of the faithful Lockheed Vega that served them so well in their flight around the world. Post is not wearing his eye patch, a telltale sign that this was regarded as a "formal" photograph.

Smithsonian Institution Photo No. A32382.

Like all of Jack Northrop's creations, the Lockheed Vega was an elegant airplane, clean of line and devoid of superfluous detail. Made entirely of wood, the Vega was truly "state-of-the-art" for its day. Few airplane designs have set so many records over such an extended period of time.

Not so complex as the Space Shuttle, the "Winnie Mae" 's instrumentation was nonetheless sophisticated for its time. Even more impressive was Post's ability to use it, especially during a period when many of the most famous fliers were unable to fly on instruments. The addition of an autopilot made a solo round-the-world flight possible.

Smithsonian Institution Photo No. A43412.

U.S. Naval Airstation, Argentia, Newfoundland.

The rock-bound shores of Harbor Grace, Newfoundland, were the starting point of many trans-Atlantic hopefuls. Not all were as successful as the "Winnie Mae," here starting the second leg of her journey by being propped into life in the classic "join-hands-and-tug-like-hell" method.

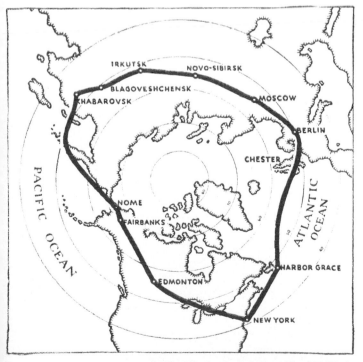

Post and Gatty selected the route for their circumglobal trip by combining the practical nonrefueled range capability of their Lockheed with available airports. It included some of the most hostile geography in the world, but they circled the earth in a record eight days, fifteen hours, and fifty-one minutes.

Smithsonian Institution Photo No. A32498-A.

Smithsonian Institution Photo No. A43412H.

Engine manufacturers were keenly conscious of the value resulting from successful flights that used their engines, and were often glad to lend entire engines, parts, and maintenance services to the leading—and usually impoverished—pilots.

One would suspect that no hands got really dirty as four of the most famous fliers in the world—Amelia Earhart, Wiley Post, Roscoe Turner, and Laura Ingalls—do a simulated autopsy on the "Winnie Mae"'s Wasp radial engine.

Lockheed Aircraft Corporation.

Fliers often depended on general good will and makeshift repair arrangements to keep their planes flying. The miners of remote Flat, Alaska, all pitched in to keep Post's 1933 solo round-the-world flight from coming to an end after a hard landing damaged "Winnie Mae"'s propeller and landing gear.

Post emerged tired but triumphant when his solo circumnavigation flight ended at Floyd Bennet Field in New York. He shaved nearly a day off the record he and Harold Gatty had set two years earlier. Entrance to and egress from the "Winnie Mae" was not easy; the cockpit was backed by fuel tanks, and Post had to climb in and out of the cockpit's upper hatch.

Wiley Post's farsighted experiments with pressure suits have been written about and commemorated in museum exhibits, yet there lingers a sense that he was only tinkering, and that his success was a product of luck. Nothing could be further from the truth; he was a pioneer, and, had he lived, he would have enjoyed immensely the routine use of pressure suits by military pilots and astronauts.

Smithsonian Institution Photo No. 77-11793.

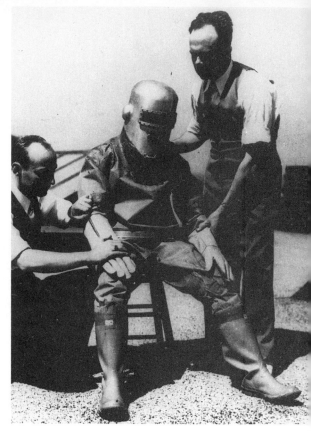

Preparation for the stratosphere flights in the ''Winnie Mae'' included the installation of a large scoop to gather air for the supercharger. *From left to right:* E. G. Mallenkopf (Post's mechanic), D. W. Smith, Wiley Post, and Paul O'Connor.

Smithsonian Institution Photo No. A41033.

Smithsonian Institution Photo No. A47708B.

A very pretty airplane for a deathtrap. This bastard combination of Lockheed Orion fuselage and Lockheed Explorer wing was the aircraft in which Post and humorist Will Rogers were killed. With a large 550-horsepower Wasp engine, controllable pitch three-bladed propeller and floats, the airplane was fatally nose-heavy.

Post took off from shallow water at Walakpi, Alaska, pulling the red-painted Orion/ Explorer into a tight climbing turn. The engine failed, and from a height of only fifty feet, the aircraft plunged into the water, killing both men instantly. The news stunned the nation.

Smithsonian Institution Photo No. A47027-D.

The cities visited by the "Winnie Mae" of Oklahoma are proudly displayed on its fuselage side. After Post's death, a grateful Congress appropriated $25,000 to purchase the plane from his widow. The aircraft was donated to the Smithsonian Institution, and may be seen at the National Air and Space Museum.

Surrounded by trophies, Post nonetheless conveyed the down-to-earth quality of the oil-field kid, somehow done up in a suit and tie.

many of the newer towns in central Siberia, towns which are mostly shipping points for ores and live stock. The country is overrun with herds. It reminded me of the Texas of my boyhood, before the oil boom hit the United States mid-continent area.

"There's a lot of soup up ahead," I shouted through the tube. "Have you any recent sights so we can go over it, or do you want to keep the ground in view?"

"Wait a minute, and I'll get a new position and see how it checks with the map markings," Gatty called back.

I stayed at that level, and before a minute went by, Harold said that he knew exactly which way Irkutsk lay. Then the thick layer of clouds slipped beneath the wheels, and we started over the top.

But the top seemed to grow higher.

"Let's go down," I said. "This stuff is getting so high that we are beginning to lose our speed. It's partly because the climb slows us, but mostly because we are up nearly 9,000 feet, and I have to keep the motor opened up wider and use more gas to get enough power to hold the cruising speed."

"I'm hanging on, so go ahead."

Gatty was a good passenger, one of the best I have ever carried. He never asked any questions or raised any disturbance about the way I pulled that ship up or knocked it down in dives that I know must have plugged his ears.

I stuck "Winnie Mae" on her nose and set myself for a drop in flying blind. That old rate-of-climb indicator just hit bottom, and the air-speed needle hit the pin the other way. It passed the 240 mark and then lopped over on its second lap. But the bank-and-turn indicator stood still, and the artificial horizon stood still, too, about halfway up the top semicircle. Never a wiggle off the true course did the "Winnie Mae" fly, and the altimeter read 6,000, then 2,500, then 1,500, when I started easing her up level again. I wanted to "feel" my way down that last stretch, for I didn't know what was underneath.

The fog thinned out toward the ground and it began to get lighter when our altimeter read 500 feet.

"Look on that map and see if there are any high spots around here," I called to Gatty. "We have been dropping for about 20 or 25 miles, so you ought to be able to pick up a location."

"We should be right near Krasnoyarsk," he said. "Gee, these names are getting hard to take again."

Evidently the railroad had made quite a bend while we were up out of sight of the ground, but Harold's figures were correct, for in a few minutes the town came up in front. It was just like the others we had seen. The Five-Year Plan had not reached it yet. The houses were old, and there was a big stockyard, or corral, near the switch yard.

Just as we came over town, we crossed the Yenisei River, which has its source south in the hills of northern Mongolia. It is just a winding stream without much traffic, apparently put there just so people would have to build bridges for the railroad to go over it. I counted three times that the rails crossed it.

The couple or more boats that were visible on the Yenisei were small and held less than a motor truck, so it couldn't have been of much use as an artery. It was wide enough, but from my view of it, it looked too shallow for larger shipping. The logs being floated downstream indicated hills to the south, so I guess it was just as well we stuck to the railroad passes on our way under the clouds.

It started to rain. I knew it was going to, because the air suddenly grew rough and gusty. Then it became smooth again as the rain began to come down. For a few moments I almost thought I was flying across Prussia and over Posen again. The rain came down in regular sheets, and I had to close all the windows. The air behind 450 horsepower certainly can get hot. It was like the steam room of a Turkish bath. When we finally pulled through into a lighter rainfall, I was wet and steaming.

"If you can get that radio going and find an interpreter, you might tell the folks at Irkutsk that I won't need a bath," I said, as soon as I could see where we were heading. "I've just been bathed by the Lord and 'Winnie Mae.' "

"It's none too dry back here, either," Gatty answered. "The ark seems to be leaking."

"Why don't you try to catch up on that sleep you lost last night?" I countered. "You can't navigate in this stuff, and I can follow the rails all the way into Irkutsk."

Harold did get a little "shut eye" in fitful 10-minute snatches that next couple of hours. With a good railroad to follow, I had no trouble navigating. The only time I can get lost following a railroad is when there are two of them or when I follow the right one the wrong way. And what pilot can't?

I rocked the plane when Irkutsk hove into sight. I knew it must be Irkutsk, because we had passed only a few isolated way stations on the line, and I hadn't heard of any other cities in those parts. In fact, I had never heard of Irkutsk until I planned a flight around the world.

The rocking brought my slumbering navigator back to life again, and he was glad, he said, that he was awake for the landing, else he might have fallen off the chair. But that wasn't why I woke him up. He had to crawl back with his chair to hold that old tail down.

We slid into a landing just as my New York-time watch said 11:50.

On the field was the largest crowd we had seen since leaving Berlin. Those Russians in the western sections of the U. S. S. R. are industrious people and have no time for the "tomfoolery" of a pair of flyers. But Irkutsk is a Russia of the older regime. The folks there have leisure, and a few hours wasted at the airport makes little difference in the long run of their lives. We needed to get information there on the location of flying fields in what now became an emergency route. Our dope was slim and of somewhat dubious accuracy.

But "hunt and ye shall find" does not apply to English-speaking Russians in Irkutsk. Our loud clamoring for somebody who spoke our own tongue fell on incomprehending ears and questioning faces.

Then the fun started. I got so many laughs ahead of Harold that I lost count. No matter how many he has had on me since, I am still ahead. As soon as he tried his French, he found several men and women who gurgled and sputtered some kind of gibberish. The poor lad was at his wit's end.

Then up stepped little Annie Polikof, prim, round, and about sixteen. For a solid minute she held Gatty spellbound with a mixture of cockney and pidgin English. The officials of *Ossoaviakhim*, who were accompanying Harold through the outskirts of the crowd on his new hunt for an interpreter, were exuberant. They had not known what it was he was after, and suddenly they thought they had found out.

I rushed over. "Let's get together on this," I said. "Maybe she knows a little American Indian sign language."

But Gatty was gradually getting his position on that tough course toward understanding. I was sure of it when he and Annie began laughing together. He told me later that he was explaining to her that the Russians understood his French all right, but that he couldn't understand theirs.

Anyhow, Annie Polikof saved the hours and maybe the

day for us. We led her firmly over to the ship. On the way, she told us in a curious kind of English that she had been born in London, but that she had left there when she was six years old.

On the whole she did a good job of telling the mechanics and airport officials what we needed, although she had plenty of difficulty in translating the technical names of tanks and other parts of the plane. But with her chatting and our pointing, cupping of hands, and counting off fingers, we three managed to get the men started on gassing the "Winnie Mae." We needed some oil, too. Our Russian oil seemed to work all right, but it thinned out pretty fast, so I had them drain the case and put in fresh stuff.

When we were given a bite to eat, I suddenly discovered that the steak of the previous night had worn off and had left a keen-edged appetite. Gatty, the cheat, said that he had eaten two biscuits on the flight over. He had cached them in his pocket the night before, while I had been paying attention to the steak. I said to him in reprimand:

"That's probably what brought you all those little visitors last night. Justice will be done."

Harold laughed and repeated the remark to Annie, who laughed and ran about telling the story to the *Ossoaviakhim* representatives. We were having a merry time while the "mechs" were giving the last finishing touches to the job under Annie's direction.

Then Harold began to figure furiously. He said that if we didn't get off quickly, we never would get even as far as Blagoveshchensk—the names got harder both to say and to spell the farther east we went—before dark. The course in between lay over Manchuria, where there was no means of communication and we knew of no possible landing place.

I'm afraid I forgot even my manners in the haste that

followed. I certainly didn't pull up in Irkutsk in the early afternoon just to sit out the rest of the day and the night there.

I hopped in and got the engine going while Gatty signed a couple of souvenirs for Annie. I waved good-by to the crowd and started taxiing out as he jumped into his seat and closed the door.

In a whirl of dust and flying bits of grass, we streaked across another rough Soviet runway and were on our way.

"What time was it there?" I called through the tube to Harold. "I want to reset my dash clock."

I got a thrill when he answered:

"Set it by your wrist watch, old boy. By daylight saving, there's just 12 hours' difference from New York time here. We are halfway home."

I felt like climbing around the outside of the ship and hitting him for not having told me sooner. But I satisfied myself by bawling him out.

We got off at 2:09 P.M., Irkutsk daylight time, and 2:09 A.M., New York time. We set the course east by south at 91°. I felt so good that I left the throttle wide open until we flew over Lake Baikal.

That was a beautiful body of water. The weather had cleared, and we were able to admire the scenery. Gatty told me through the tube that Lake Baikal was associated with the first thing he had ever heard about Russia. It seems that in his early days at school he had learned that in one of the campaigns of the then recent Russo–Japanese War the Russian troops were marched across this lake on the ice when the troop traffic proved too heavy for the railroads.

It took us about an hour to leave the lake behind. A few minutes afterward we crossed a small range of high mountains and a wide valley with the greenest grass I have ever seen. The valley was flat, and the Kurba River flowed through the center of it. At 3:43 Harold had me alter the course to 94° and a few minutes later, to 98°. As we barged fast over Chita, in the foothills of the Yablonovoi Mountains, about 120 miles from the Manchurian line, he altered it again to 100°. It was then 4:42 by my watch.

Then we started a climb up over that wooded range. The growth was so luxuriant that I wondered how the weather ever turned cold enough to freeze Lake Baikal hard enough to support an army.

I was in a hurry as I dropped down the east slope in a dive to pick up some of the time lost in the climb. We started making tracks, and I kept the air speed at 160 instead of throttling back to the regular cruising speed of 145 or 150. The ship trimmed all right, so I had no extra amount of fuel burning—that is, no appreciable amount.

In a scant half hour we crossed into Manchuria, where the nomad bands of North China are supposed to have roamed for centuries. Somebody with a lot of money should buy that country. It looks as if it would grow anything, and the terrain is perfect. I found out later that the weather is of the wet-and-dry-season sort, but then it looks so nice in the dry season, and one wouldn't have to live there all year 'round. I'd like to be a personal pilot for the man who bought it.

We plunged across that Manchurian land for the next 260 or 270 miles, and never a sign of habitation did we see. From the time we first crossed the Amur River at 6:29 to our second crossing of it at about 8:30, at the point where it turns south near Blagoveshchensk, there wasn't a single sight that might lead us to believe that anybody had ever been there. I'd be willing to bet that you could have a lot of fun in that neighborhood with a good pair of guns.

When we crossed the Amur the second time, I had my work cut out for me. Just as it gets light out there early in the morning, so I found that darkness sets in early. It comes swiftly and without the warning of a long twilight. To make matters worse, it had been raining all day in Blagoveshchensk, and the sky was still overcast. I picked up the town all right, but I couldn't locate the airport, which was supposed to have been marked out by oil flares.

Gatty caught a string of lights down along the east bank of the river and called to me. I flew around in a circle a couple of times and then saw them myself, so I tore across. My gas was beginning to run a little low, but I hadn't had to turn on that last 20-minutes' supply yet.

I think that if I had swept over that field a few more times, I would have thought it was a lake. All I could see was water. The flares reflected across what we knew must be the airport with just the same sort of widening beam that the moon throws on a lake. I knew I was in for a trick landing.

"Get as far back as you can. Hold your instruments so they won't break. Set yourself for a jolt and hang on like hell," I called back in the quietest tone I could muster under the circumstances.

I felt Harold move back as I slid in over the Amur River and cut the gun. Night landings had never bothered me before, but when all the lights you have give you merely an outline of a rectangle and then shine on only water, there isn't much you can do but feel your way to the ground and trust to luck.

I stuck the tail down as I had done at Harbor Grace and brought the ship in on the throttle at about 900 revolutions a minute. Old "Winnie Mae" may never learn how little confidence Wiley had that night. I mushed her down until I thought the ground must surely be sloping downhill toward me, and kept my hand on the throttle to get away fast if a hump should hide the dim flares on the other end.

I started moving the stick around like a coffee spoon, feeling the controls. Then I saw a half-dry spot and held the ship off until I could hit it. I nearly did hit it, too. Just missed it by about 10 feet.

We thought we were in a seaplane. Spray flew all over the place. Mud clogged up the pants on the wheels. Almost as soon as we touched, lightly as I could hold the ship up with the motor still running a little above the idling point, which gave us a wee bit too much speed, I felt that oozy mud. No bounce, no run, and the determination to hold that tail down, come what might.

We rolled less than 400 feet from our landing, at a speed which I estimate must have been close to 80 miles an hour. As long as the ship kept moving, we were all right, but I couldn't keep her going. She got heavier and heavier, and when I tried to turn, I felt her left wheel sink.

My heart sank with that wheel!

There I sat. The 10-day schedule of "the fast boys, Post and Gatty," seemed to me to be at an end—in a mudhole in the last 300 miles of Siberia.

What a break!

=11=

BLAGOVESHCHENSK TO KHABAROVSK

(GATTY)

I NEVER FELT SO SORRY FOR ANYONE IN MY LIFE AS I DID for Wiley when "Winnie Mae" stopped in the mud at Bla-goveshchensk. It was the end, too, for me, but I was used to disappointment by that time. Hadn't I been well out over the Pacific with Bromley, only to be forced back?

I slopped out through the mud as a few timid people, well protected from the weather, came across the field in hip boots. There was still a light drizzle. When I tumbled out of the door and over the edge of the sill, the long step made me drop on one knee in the water. It was fully two inches deep, and the ooze underneath was six inches to a foot thick.

With my feet making strange sucking sounds, audible even to my motor-deafened ears, I struggled around the struts, holding on so I wouldn't slip again. Wiley was crouched on his haunches, with his hand down under the edge of the tire, trying to find a rock or something that might keep the ship from settling any farther.

Just then a Ford sloshed through the mire with the *Os-*

126

soaviakhim men in it. They had two Danish telegraph operators with them, both of whom spoke good English, and we tried to negotiate a push. Somebody produced a rope, which we tied to the tow ring on the left axle of the ship and to the rear of the car.

Wiley, tired as he was, got the motor going again, and the Ford and the Wasp worked in unison to get that wheel up on firm ground. The wheels of the light car merely spun helplessly in the mud, tossing out a black fountain. "Winnie Mae" began to rock herself deeper into the bog as the vibration and sporadic movements disturbed what little soil was holding her afloat in that sea of ooze.

We shouted, we raved, and we ranted, until I thought we would become hysterical. At last one of the airport officials announced (the Danes passed the word on to us) that he had sent for a tractor. He suggested that we go to town and sleep, and said that he would have a gang of laborers with the tractor there by morning to get us out.

We had been in that bog for more than an hour. We were wet through and covered with slime. I was hungry, but I wouldn't admit it before Wiley. After much persuasion we at last decided to abandon the ship for the time being and to go into the administration office to think things over.

We used the Ford for a ferryboat to get to the office of the commandant. The farther away from the ship we drove, the wetter and softer the ground became, until it seemed as if Wiley had picked out the one spot on that field that would keep "Winnie Mae" out of the K-boat class of submarines.

But the climax to the greatest serio-comic situation I have ever seen came when we walked into the office.

When I looked at Wiley, I just had to give way to my feelings. I was bedraggled myself, but I doubt if anyone ever looked as funny as he did then.

He waddled into the lighted room, dragging one foot behind the other. His clothes stuck to him in queer folds. His face was spattered with mud, and he wore that dejected look of comic pathos with which Charlie Chaplin established the reputation that brought him fame and fortune. And the muddy water from the field dripped to a pool about his indefinitely shaped feet.

As I burst out laughing, he glared at me as if he had rehearsed the act. At first he couldn't see anything funny in the break in our luck. Then he saw me. I must have looked just as bad to him as he did to me, for he grinned with that inscrutable facial contortion that only people under physical or emotional stress can make natural.

The Russians were far too polite even to smile at our discomfiture. They chattered excitedly among themselves, and from their motions I could see the "Winnie Mae" being pulled out of the bog by each individual there. Some of them looked strong enough to do it, too.

The two Danes, Jacobsen and Nelsen, were the most harassed men in the group. They were trying hard to establish a line of communication between Wiley and the commandant.

But when the Russians, ten strong in the tight ring around them, heard their speeches, each tried to voice his own particular plan independent of all the others. Consequently, nobody heard anybody else, and the volume of sound gradually rose from the first low mumblings of two or three to the crescendo of a huge chorus. The two Danes, as the high tenors, outdid everybody else in their efforts to predominate, but failed.

Outside, the drizzle continued. The water was seeping silently to earth like a quiet but persistent victor. I could hardly help looking through the open window and admiring its apparent triumph. Wiley walked over, too, and together we sat on the window sill and watched the rain come down. He was so drowsy that he began to nod. I was none too alert myself, but my own nervous reactions and a concentrated rage—suppressed, under the circumstances—kept me from even thinking of sleep.

Outside, the rain, and inside, the proletariat doing its best to be heard. When we had moved a little apart from the crowd, most of the men had followed us. They couldn't talk to us or we to them, but there was something sympathetic about their attitude. First on one foot and then on the other, they stood around in a little half circle and just looked miserable for us.

"Well, I don't think we'll have much trouble with the navigation for the next few hours," I chanced at Wiley.

"No, and we can be roommates in the poorhouse, or maybe the nut house, if we don't get out of here by morning," he returned.

With that sweet morsel of humor to think over, I decided that we had better try golden silence if we wanted to keep up the morale of the around-the-world-flight personnel.

There is no denying they were low hours for both of us. The day had been even more grueling on Wiley than on me. Despite my lack of sleep, I seemed to see things as they were.

"We'll get out all right," I assured him.

When the crowd had moved over toward us, the two Danish friends were left talking alone to the commandant. Suddenly, as if to fulfill my astonishing platitude, they strode through the circle.

The commandant shouted some peremptory order, which drew the crowd away from us. Then the Danes quietly told us that arrangements had been made to obtain a farm tractor from about a 3-hour tractor-crawl away. They said that there was no use in our sitting at the airport, and they invited us to their own homes to wait for the ship to be pulled clear. The prospect of food, a bed, and a bath, was too much for me to resist, and I accepted with no small amount of enthusiasm.

Not so Wiley, however, who outlined his sensible plans. We expected the tractor there in 3 or 4 hours. It would take another hour or more to fuel the ship and get it ready for the 2-hour jump to Khabarovsk. Then we could hurry the start for Nome. If we stood by and were ready, we might not lose much time. Besides, he said he wanted to be around when the laborers were hooking things onto the "Winnie Mae's" landing gear.

But Wiley insisted that I go with the Danes and bring him back something to eat. I did.

I was hardly outside the airport gate when I realized the sense of Post's program of staying at the field. It was an hour's back-breaking ride in a jerking two-wheeled droshky to the homes of my two new friends.

At the end of the hour's ride, however, I was fully rewarded. Those two employees of the Danish telegraph company that held a line through Russia and Siberia to the Orient were the most hospitable people I have ever met. Their wives were more than kind to me. They had a nice hot meal ready for me so soon after I arrived that I hardly had time to enjoy my first real hot tub since leaving Roosevelt Field.

The food was imported from Denmark. Sausages, some kind of Danish vegetable combination, and coffee put me back on my feet. I even became alert enough to ply the men with questions as to life in Russia under the new regime. The conversation was so interesting that my new Danish friends almost had to force me to lie down and get some sleep. How little I envied Wiley when I sank into that downy bed!

Nearly 2 hours later Jacobsen shook me awake and told me it was time to go back to the field. I never was so near to giving up the ghost of the flight as at that moment. I wanted to go back into that bed and stay there for a week. But the thought of Wiley out there at the field brought me through, and I reluctantly donned my coat. Perhaps I even had a little spring in my step as I walked through the door-yard of the neat cottage, carrying a good basket of "spare parts for Wiley's soul" (to quote Mr. Jacobsen), which Mrs Nelsen had packed for him.

The rain had stopped, and a light wind had already whipped the earth road to a respectable dryness. Back we went, via the droshky, to the airport.

There I learned that immediately after I had left, Wiley had tramped through the mud and water to the ship. He had climbed into my seat, and there we found him, the chair tilted back, his head on his shoulder. He had been sleeping the entire 4 hours.

The ground outside the plane was beginning to get firm enough to walk on with comfort. It was thick black soil, but it must have had a natural subsoil of loam or some other substance, for it was draining rapidly.

The tractor was still "on the way." We took the horse from the droshky and borrowed another horse from one of the Russians. When the engine started to roar, the poor horses were so frightened that it seemed as if the traces would break before "Winnie Mae" was pried loose from that hole which she had dug the night before. We had to give up. The horses couldn't pull the heavy machine through that leaden soil.

It was another 5 hours, during which Wiley and I got in a little more sleep, before the ground had dried hard enough to give the poor animals foothold. The tractor had not yet arrived. Then with everyone either straining on ropes or pushing on the fuselage, old "Winnie Mae" came out with a great heave.

It was 12 hours and 21 minutes after we had bogged down that we finally said good-by to our friends and helpers and were off again. By New York time it was 9:21 P.M., but it was nearly noon in Blagoveshchensk.

The flight over to Khabarovsk was but 363 miles, and, aside from crossing the lower ends of the Bureya and Vanda ranges of the Little Khingan Mountains, no outstanding events stick in my memory.

The only two entries in the ship's log on the Greenwich-time schedule are:

"Took off Blagoveshchensk, 1:21."

"Landed Khabarovsk, 3:56."

We had a good wind, and the railroad was almost constantly in sight, so there was little navigating to do. I let my thoughts run in retrospect on the charm of the Danish people who had befriended us, and in prospect over the hardest, most experimental, and longest flight of the trip, which was yet to come. We were soon to be headed for Solomon, Alaska, 2,441 miles by the shortest route, a route fraught with the difficulties of over-water flying, fog, and unknown mountains.

12

JUNE 29

FROM KHABAROVSK TO FAIRBANKS

(POST)

COVERING 2,441 MILES IN 3¼ HOURS LESS THAN NOTHING IS A trick. Some scientist figured it out after the earth was proved to be round. I had it impressed on me when we took off from Khabarovsk at 6:56 Monday night, June 29, and arrived at Solomon, Alaska, at 2:48 in the afternoon of the same Monday, June 29. That was more amazing than the yarn about Columbus standing the egg on its point.

But I am getting a little ahead of my story. When we landed the ship at Khabarovsk at 2 o'clock Sunday afternoon, we felt that our battle was won. I slipped in carefully. Perhaps I was a bit "ground shy" after that incident at Blagoveshchensk. We rolled to a stop, and I taxied over to the hangar. Then I let the stick drop out of my fingers, certain that we would more than make good our boast to return to Roosevelt Field in 10 days.

"We'll be home within a week of our start," were my first words to Gatty after I recovered my hearing.

"Not unless we get going fast," he said.

I was tired, and I decided that we should take every

precaution before we started on the last extra-long hop. Coming across the steppes and plains of Siberia, we had not considered weather reports as an important factor in our decisions. But now we had plenty of time, and I felt that we ought to get what weather reports we could over the route we were to follow from here on, or at least for as far as our heavy load was to last. When we would begin to fly light from partially exhausted fuel tanks, I would not mind flying blind.

Harold did his best to collect some weather data, especially on wind directions, while I started in on the ship. "Winnie Mae" had received even less care than ourselves since she had spanked her wing against the wet air at Roosevelt Field 5½ days before. Pilots may fly when they have rheumatism, navigators may guide without maps, but unless airplanes are given a certain amount of personal attention, they will become perverse.

I began by going to work on the old girl's heart. I knew that all the valves were working and that no murmurs had made it leaky, but I was certain that there was something I could do to improve "Winnie Mae's" condition and to reassure her that her days of hard work were about at an end.

We had carried a half set of spare plugs with us, so I took out the lower four plugs, which I thought might have become pretty well oil-soaked from that thinning Russian lubricant. They looked all right, but just to make sure, I stuck the new ones in. Then I swung the prop and felt the compression on each cylinder. Not that there were any bad leaks (if there had been, I should have heard them in flight), but my hands are much more sensitive than my ear, and I wanted to be sure. To my delight, everything checked up as well as on the morning we had taken off. I had lost a little time, but I had gained plenty of confidence.

Meanwhile Gatty came back with his weather report.

From a radio announcement made by the observatory at Tokyo he had learned that a low-pressure area with billowy cloud banks was clearing away from our route. The Japanese weather doctors said that the low was then driving east from the Sea of Okhotsk. However, another smaller area was headed northwest through the Sea of Japan. This might give us head winds and make the visibility on our path poor.

"What about getting off tonight just before dark, and trying to beat it through?" I suggested.

Harold looked over the charts with me. We had a scheduled detour and fuel stop at Petropavlovsk, on the southeastern tip of the Kamchatka Peninsula. This would take us over a route more than 200 miles longer than the Great Circle Track and make the possibility of running into that Sea of Japan storm just so much greater.

"What do you think of the chances of getting off from here with the full load?" Harold asked.

I looked out at the runway, and after some consideration and a recollection of Harbor Grace, I said, "If we get a good wind from the right direction, we can make it."

"Then let's do it, and go straight through to Solomon."

I would like to have known a little more about those winds before making any snap judgments, but I gave the order to fill up the tanks, anyhow. We were badly in need of sleep, so Harold and I left for the hotel. There were some crowds, but the city had only 5,000 population, so we weren't bothered much.

Three hours later we came back to the field, and one look at the wind sock made me regret I had been so hasty in having the tanks loaded heavily. The wind was straight across the runway, and it would have been useless even to have tried getting off. It was still Sunday at Khabarovsk, but getting dark.

I had a few misgivings that we might have another enforced wait like that at Roosevelt Field. But we could always take out some of the fuel load to get off in a cross wind and then refuel at Petropavlovsk, as we had originally planned.

The desire for more sleep softened our disappointment somewhat, and we went into one of the hangars. There we stretched out on a couple of cots and dropped off to sleep. We slept until the next afternoon. When we awoke, wind conditions had changed enough to make the take-off with full load possible.

A light wind from the north was slightly across "Winnie Mae's" path down the runway. At 6:56 P.M. local time, 8:56 A.M. London time, and 4:56 A.M. New York daylight time, we took off. The good old ship flew off in better shape than she had at Harbor Grace.

We set our course at 52° and started up over the 3-hour run along the Amur River to the Tatar Strait. Although the weather was clear, we held the ship down to 75 feet above the water all the way in order to make better time against the wind. I was a little uncertain as to whether it was too strong to fight on a nonstop run to Alaska, but Harold was keeping a close check on the ground speed.

The river wound through swamps that must have been alive with pests. Just about 10 o'clock, we saw an old side-wheeler paddling its way down to Nikolaevsk, which is located at the delta of the ever-widening stream. We lost it from view as we cut one of the corners between bends in the stream. We flew so low that the trees—one could call them big bushes—skimmed under the wheels.

"This sticking down low has reduced the speed of that head wind to about 8 miles an hour. We've been averaging 140 ground speed," Harold said.

"If it stays that way and doesn't get any stronger, keep to the north, and we'll go straight through to Solomon," I answered. "But be sure to get a good check on our ground speed before we head out over the Okhotsk. We'll not have any more chances for fuel after we pass Kamchatka."

As we flew low above the river, we frightened the natives who were plying along in sampans. I suppose we must have looked rather terrifying to them in that last few minutes of daylight. It probably was the first time they had ever seen an airplane. The Russian air lines do not extend across that area. The planes which go to eastern Siberia come through from Yakutsk, and their courses lie nearly 1,000 miles north.

At 11:39 by Greenwich time we left the marshy land which is formed by the streams running down off the Sikhota Alin. This mountain range had towered above us to the right of the course for 2 hours. The country was one of the wildest sections we saw all the way around, especially where we ran out beyond the end of the mountain range to the west coast of Sakhalin Island, toward the Sea of Okhotsk.

From here on it was hard flying. As the tip of Sakhalin Island passed behind, Gatty made his last check on our speed. The time had come for the decision. Should we go over the Great Circle Track to Solomon? Or should we strike out due east for the lower tip of Kamchatka and set the ship down at Petropavlovsk, where we could get more gas and a rest?

Despite the work of flying the ship for hours so low that it had to be "flown every second" along the way, I was not the least bit tired.

"We are still holding 140 miles an hour," Harold said, and went on to analyze the first 4 hours of the run. "We came 557 miles up to 12:55, and from a sight I just took, in about 21 minutes we should cross position 2 at 51° 56′ N. and 140° E., 606 miles from Khabarovsk."

"At that rate, we ought to be able to make it right through," I answered back over my shoulder, as soon as

I had checked the figures on a little slide rule I had on the dash. "And we should get to Solomon in about 18 hours."

"That checks with my calculations," Gatty said. "Keep well to the left and hold your course at 62° until I get a chance to figure the drift."

Being over water now, the Okhotsk Sea, I pulled up to 1,500 feet. We were crabbing into the wind, but not hard, and the rudder was only about 2 or 3 points off normal straight position.

"Allow 8° for left drift," said Harold, surprising me. "The wind must have changed on that climb. It's east-southeast now and more on the nose. That might bring clouds. We must be getting near that bank forecast by the weather reports."

The weather began to grow thicker every minute as we tore across that sea in the darkest hours of the moonless night. By the time we were out over the middle of it, at 150° E. Long., I was forced down to within a few feet of the water. A few bumps warned me that side gusts were hitting the wing. One cocked the ship up a little, so I had to give up trying to keep the water in sight. The gusts were so violent that I might have been flying through a mountain pass like some I had run across, which actually threw the ship momentarily out of control. But I knew there was nothing except water underneath.

Ordinarily, flight over water is smoother than over land. The air temperature is more constant, and the curvature of the ground is absent, so the air currents have straight paths in which to circulate.

Nevertheless, I had heard and read a few things about typhoons and queer storms in the section of the world north from Japan. I wasn't going to take any chances.

"I'm going upstairs and fly this stuff blind," I called to Gatty.

And blind it was. I pulled up carefully to 1,500 feet and

leveled off. Then I settled back to that vigil of watching my three instruments. The bank-and-turn, the rate-of-climb, and the artificial horizon all settled themselves slowly to the centers of their respective ranges, and I made every motion with the controls slowly and deliberately.

Relaxation is the best moderator of the tendency to be erratic in flying blind. I let the ship fly itself as much as possible, and only occasionally during the next hour did I have to do anything but sit back and take life easy. Once I trimmed the ship a little down at the tail when the rate-of-climb indicator insisted on showing a shallow dive of about 50 feet a minute.

The light on the instrument board flickered and went out, but as all the dials were luminous, I found that I could see them better without the light, once my eye became accustomed to the darkness.

At the end of the hour, 16 o'clock by navigation time, we ran out of the thick fog under a black ceiling. I slid the window back to get a little more air and pushed my face over near it. Something stung me. I put my hand out carefully and pulled it back in a hurry. It was hailing. Those hailstones cut like shot when you are going 155 miles an hour, which was what my indicator showed.

"What's the temperature back there?" I asked Harold.

He had an extra thermometer with its bulb sticking out in the open. We used it for a check on the remote pyrometer bulb, whose indicator was on the board before me.

"It says 44°," he answered. "Are you watching for ice?"

"Well, I just got a sample of hail, and wanted to make sure," was my reply. "It seems pretty warm for hail, but it may be colder up higher."

Suddenly the hail changed to rain. And such rain you never saw! In the darkness it seemed as if it were slightly luminous, for I could see the propeller track although I could see nothing else outside. It might have been my imagination or some illusion, but it seemed strange to me.

I have flown through tropical showers on the mail runs in Mexico and thought that they might be described as the heaviest waterfalls in the world. But this rain over the Sea of Okhotsk was so heavy that it reminded me of that joke about the pilot who was flying an amphibian through the rain.

"It was raining so hard that I just pulled up the wheels and landed right there, 6,000 feet above the city," he said.

Another joke that I thought of then was the one told by Jeb Smith, who had flown through one of those Mexican cloudbursts. He said he had noticed some funny-looking lumps gathering on the wing, had reached out, and had pulled in a fish.

I relayed those two stories back to Harold, but I don't think he appreciated them. Perhaps he was hungry again, and didn't like fish.

Just after we had run into the rain, I pulled up sharply. There seemed to be a break in the clouds, because the sky was black, then light, while farther ahead it seemed darker and more forbidding than ever.

I leveled off at 6,000 feet and was surprised to see that the pyrometer read 46°. We were then flying, as nearly as I could see, between two layers of clouds. Every so often it would grow light enough to look down at what appeared to be the top of the rain bank. Overhead, billowy masses of fog seemed to stick down at us. For 1 hour and 40 minutes we flew intermittently in and above the fog. Then, through a sudden hole in the clouds above, Gatty got a quick sight and located our position near the halfway mark at 60° 32' N. Lat. and 160° E. Long. We had been out only 8 hours and 44 minutes, so we knew we must have been making better time than on the first part of the trip, above the Amur River.

"We ought to be over the Kamchatka Peninsula now," Harold said.

"Do you think you could pick up a landmark if we went down through this mess?" I asked.

"Try it. But take it as slowly as you can after you get down to 3,000. The map shows elevations, and I don't know how good they are," he warned.

So we dropped through to 3,000 feet and suddenly came out under a high-riding layer of clouds. It was beginning to grow light already, and we could distinguish land. I still held up the nose a bit above a steep dive, but it cost me an effort. It felt good to be able to see land after flying blind over water.

We were doomed to disappointment, though. The maps Gatty had obtained from the Russians showed varied colors for elevations in the mountains of Kamchatka up to 500 meters—1,500 feet or thereabout. But as we flew along at 3,000, we were sneaking up on higher ground all the time. One snow-capped peak which stood out on our right must have been at least 4,000 feet, for it seemed to stick right into the clouds.

"Say! That isn't on the map at all," Gatty squealed. "Either these elevations are all wrong or our altimeter is haywire."

"Well, they don't have snow on mountains at 1,500 feet, and it is only 37° on my thermometer, so I'm inclined to believe the altimeter. It might be a little out from a falling barometer, but not that much," I answered.

As we flew along without finding a break in the country, I asked, "How much of this rocky stuff is there? How wide is this land?"

"About 210 miles where our course crosses," Harold replied.

"These things are getting too close to the ceiling for my

comfort and peace of mind," I announced. "Isn't there any narrower place?"

"Both north and south," came the answer. "If we want to alter the course, we had better take the north side, because it won't take us so far from the regular track."

"How much out of the way will it be?" I sent back through the tube. "We have some leeway now because we are making better time than I thought we would."

"Maybe an hour or a little over," replied Harold.

"Navigate me, kid," I commanded. "And take the place where that map shows the least altitude at the highest point. Take what they call the peaks for the passes, and we ought to be nearly right."

"Steer about north by east then, at 10°," he said, "and as soon as you pick up the coast of this land, follow it along. There are two towns to the north, and we can plot a course up there which will be over the mountains for only about 20 miles."

"Righto!" I snapped, bringing the nose around. A big fellow slipped across the horizon from left to right.

"Wow! I'm sure glad we had a ceiling here," I sent over my shoulder. "That would be hard to take if we got it tangled up in the prop."

Gatty looked out at the snowy top of the mountain and agreed with me.

In about 20 minutes we picked up a small village about 2 miles from the coast. From the direction of the shore line and the position of the settlement Harold identified it on the map as Tigil. The name didn't mean a thing to me. It might as well have been the Cape of Good Hope for all I cared, just as long as he kept navigating me somewhere away from those mountains.

That country was wild enough to scare Daniel Boone. Nothing but rocks, trees, and more rocks. I made a mental note to recommend the district to a couple of my friends in the New York Explorer's Club, who were looking for some place to explore.

Gatty's position-finding by the "maybe-it's-right" map seemed to check up all right on the coast. In about 23 minutes we came to another village, with boats, a dock, and a water front. He said it was Palana, and that we should turn east again.

Looking east, I saw the tops of the mountains which now formed a ridge about 10 or 15 miles inland. They were pretty high, and in the early morning light they looked "not so good."

"Swing around to 97° for about 40 minutes," Gatty instructed. "I want to get a position from the sky if we get over that stratum of fog, in jumping the mountains."

The mountains there were lower and didn't have any snow. There seemed to be about a 1,000-foot clearance between the tops and the base of the clouds.

"What do you want to go up through that junk for?" I asked.

"Well, we've been doing a lot of detouring for the past half hour, and I don't want to take the locations shown on this map as accurate enough to start a new course from. If the elevations are all haywire, then the rest of the map must have been made from a free-hand drawing or something. We haven't any extra gas to go looking for Alaska, have we?"

I needed no further argument. My trouble was that I had thought a map was a map.

"O.K.," I shouted. "Hang on, your chair is coming up to meet you."

I dived the ship slightly to gather a little speed. Then I yanked her back on her tail, and we started up. When we passed the first of the peaks, all wooded and deserted-looking, we were already letting the clouds lick the top of the wing. A brilliant light nearly blinded me as we came through the top of the layer, which was thin and white where it met the morning. I put on sunglasses.

Gatty got a moon-and-sun line fix and we started going on a new course to Solomon. Once he got our position, I dropped back through the clouds. I knew we were beyond the mountains, so I didn't care a bit how fast we barged through the bottom.

We came out over a third little town, labeled Karaga on the misleading map. Then we followed a course about 50 miles seaward from the coast line of Anadir, the most easterly province of Siberia. From time to time for the next 2 hours we had a few fleeting glimpses of the shore and a high range of mountains inland. The weather began to get a little spotty after that, and the coast line swerved away from us to the north as we headed across Bering Sea for St. Lawrence Island, which was to be our first sight of land belonging to the good old U.S.A. since we had stuck "Winnie Mae's" nose toward the Bay of Fundy off from Bar Harbor, Maine, just about a week before.

The air began to fog up, and the temperature took a sudden drop. We came down within a scant 25 feet of the water, and as we rounded our course to the left, to keep close to land, we crossed over the current which flows down from the Arctic through Bering Strait, and then clings to the Siberian shore. First in little patches and then in huge crags, the broken ice was floating down to melt in the warmer waters of the south.

Flying low was not safe through that area, even at our altitude of 25 feet. I had visions of coming on a high berg in the suddenness of a quarter-mile visibility and a 150-mile-an-hour speed.

I didn't want to fly high through that fog, though, unless I pulled well up over the top, where the air would be cold enough to prevent ice from forming on the wings. I stuck it out at about 150 feet as long as I could, and we must have been well beyond the current when a small hole revealed clear water again, somewhere off Cape Navarin.

It was at some point in there that we passed from about 11 A.M. Tuesday, June 30, into 11 A.M. Monday, June 29, by crossing the International Date Line on the 180th meridian.

For the first time in my life I had a chance to live a day over again, and I had no choice as to how I was to live it, either. If I were given all my former days to relive, I should never devote any hours of them to duplicating the 3 hours which followed.

Fog, rain, fog, and more rain. We thundered through the mist and drizzle. I would gladly have swapped that day's gain on Old Man Time for an hour, or even a few minutes, of direct sunlight.

We found a slight break over Cape Kukuliak on St. Lawrence Island, and Harold took a bearing from it.

"Gee," he said, "it sure feels good to take a bearing from a set of maps in which you have confidence. We go from here in on such reliable ones that we can almost dispense with the sextant and watches. Keep a little to the left. We can swing in behind Nome and come out over Solomon with a right turn."

But the fog closed in again. I looked at the fuel gauges and found that we still had 2 hours' gasoline.

I didn't like the elevations in behind Nome so I called to Harold, "I had better pull up a bit. How high are those Kigluaik Mountains?"

"Oh, they run about 2,000 feet," he answered. "I checked them when I was figuring out the Bromley flight. But better take about 4,000, because our altimeter may be a little out. I don't know what the barometric pressure is down there now."

"Winnie Mae" stuck her nose at the sky beyond the fog, and just for good measure I let her have her way until she leveled off again at 6,000. With that margin we were out above the fog.

The air had the weirdest light I have ever flown through. It was early afternoon, but all the clouds below threw shadows across those clouds lower than themselves. It wasn't the shadows that gave the peculiar effect as much as the angles at which they were cast and the oddities of their coloring.

Through a thin wisp of fog we glimpsed water. Then Sledge Island flitted by under the fog veil.

"Don't let her get too far to the south. It's only 28 miles to Nome and less than 70 to Solomon. In half an hour pull up and circle high, and we'll look for a hole," Harold called.

So at 9:15 by my New York-time watch, I pulled the ship wide around to the right and steered about 2 miles southeast. Then I pulled her up on her left wing tip and put her through a series of steep banks. I saw another one of those floating veils of thin mist and dropped the ship at it, coming out of the bank with a long dive. I shut the throttle, but the dive was so fast that the engine hardly slackened its speed, although the roar stopped. We blasted a hole through that thin place in the curtain which was hiding Alaska from our view. We came out of the bottom of the cloud like a plummet, and I eased the stick back slowly, so as not to put too much strain on the wings or tail.

At first we could hardly see what was below. The altimeter read 2,400 feet. Then the white line of the beach stood out. Next, Fort Davis outlined itself, and as I turned idly about until I could get my bearings and sight working together, I saw, east from Cape Nome, that long thin island on which we were to land. Norton Sound was still under the darkened light of the overcast sky, and the weird light was breaking through in long oblique shafts. The water was dappled in varying shades of blue and gray.

I spotted the beach and flew over it once to get a line on the best way to approach. I was to make a cross-wind landing, so it mattered little which side I came in from. Seeing the wind slightly from the eastern sector, I closed the throttle tight, and slipped down for a glide onto the sand from the west.

The beach was a good landing field, although it was somewhat soft. As we touched, the tail rose a little as the deep sand swirled up around the pants of the wheels and made a natural though unreliable brake. At last we stopped, and the idling motor throbbed like a tired runner. The oil was almost as thin as the gas, and the fuel tanks were nearly empty.

It was so early in the afternoon, 2:45 P.M. in Alaska, that we made up our minds to hasten the refueling and to get as far as Fairbanks before we slept. If the runway at Nome had been long enough, we would have gone there for an overnight stop.

With 100 gallons of fuel aboard, we started to take off. Taxiing back along the beach, the ship started to sink into the sand. With a quick thrust I banged the throttle open to pull her through it before we were stuck. But all I succeeded in doing was to boost the tail up into the air. With a loud slap the propeller cut a hole in the sand and bent both tips on the blades. I cut the emergency switch just in time to keep "Winnie Mae" from making an exhibition of herself by standing on her nose. That would have been fatal to our hopes.

I jumped out and surveyed the damage. With a wrench, a broken-handled hammer, and a round stone, I drew out the tips of the blades so they would at least fan the air in the right direction.

But misfortunes never come singly. Harold was swinging the prop for a prime with the switch cut to restart the hot engine. He called "all clear" to me, and I switched on and whirled the booster. One of the hot charges of gasoline caught on the upstroke of the piston, and with a back fire the Wasp kicked. The propeller flew out of Harold's hands, and the blade opposite smacked his shoulder before he could jump clear of the track. He dropped like a log. It was fortunate, to say the least, that it was the flat side of the blade which hit him, though it gave him a bad bruise and a wrenched back. If the prop had been going the other way, he might have been sliced in two.

Like a major, Harold climbed in as soon as he had recovered his senses, and we took off for Fairbanks. I was as cautious as I had ever been on that run along the shifting sands of Solomon beach. Luck was with me, and we got away without misfortune No. 3. I hope we didn't leave it behind for the next bird who lands there!

Flying at 68°, we plunged through a few small clouds and in a few minutes picked up the Yukon River. We wound in and out through the hills to the fork at Tanana and then followed the south branch, the Tanana River, which winds about on the way to Fairbanks. Our compass swung through nearly half its points on that route, and we ambled along with the river in sight most of the time, covering the scant 510 miles air line in the comparatively slow time of 3 hours and 6 minutes.

At Fairbanks we left "Winnie Mae" to the tender care of the crack mechanics of the Alaskan Airways. They were to wipe her down, refuel, and oil her. Much to our surprise, they had a gleaming new propeller just our size. Our spirits were much better when we left the landing field for a short 3 or 4 hours of sleep at the local hotel.

Our trip was nearly over. Success was within our grasp. A year before, the 2-day flight from Fairbanks to New York might have seemed a large undertaking. Now, with all we had been through, it seemed like nothing more than a training flight.

When we turned out the light to catch our "shut eye," we both agreed that nothing short of fire, earthquake, or some other unforeseen catastrophe beyond the control of the firm Post, Gatty & Co., could stop us from setting a record which should withstand the snipers and sharpshooters of aviation for some time to come.

13

JUNE 30

FAIRBANKS TO EDMONTON

(GATTY)

TWO MORE HOPS AND HOME. FROM FAIRBANKS ON, WE BEGAN to feel the pace. Wiley didn't act all in, but he looked it. Somehow the 1,300 miles to Edmonton and the next 1,800 or so miles to New York seemed like the longest part of the trip. The "Winnie Mae" and her engine, however, acted just as spry as they had when we took off from Roosevelt Field, 6 or 7 days—months, it seemed—back.

We stayed in Fairbanks 6 hours, lacking a minute, and, needless to say, we didn't spend much time in looking over the town. Freshened by our rest we started out, and the Lockheed poked her white prow and new prop up over the mountains, dark with virgin fir on their lower slopes, rocky, forbidding, and cold at the tops. It was no country to be forced down in, but we didn't expect to be forced down. Near those ore-filled mountains compasses were not too dependable, so on this leg both Wiley and I studied the maps closely.

We caught a good tail wind across the peaks and bowled over the rough country out of U.S. territory and into the

Canadian Yukon—about 300 miles—in an hour and a half.

We had caught up with Monday, and now Tuesday was catching up with us. On that flight over the mountains we gained an hour, in addition to our flying time, each 400 or 500 miles we traveled.

We swung east over the Klondike country and cut across the Canadian Divide about 100 miles south of Dawson. The crags of the Canadian Rockies crept across our panorama. Old, abandoned mines and tiny settlements rolled slowly under the nose of the ship like a moving drop scene in a theater.

I left the navigation of the plane pretty much to the horse sense of Wiley. I simply traced our course on the map so we would have a constant check on our position in case we ran into bad weather and could no longer follow landmarks.

When we had taken off from Fairbanks at 3:25 A.M. we had had a last look at the early northern dawn for which the Klondike is so famous. In the eerie light the mountains had stood out, unreal and grotesque, like a challenge from the gods to our progress and a taunt to the indomitable mechanical spirit of the "Winnie Mae."

Just 1 hour and 50 minutes after leaving Fairbanks, we roared across the town of White River and an hour later passed the Yukon near its source. Swift mountain streams, ever-changing elevations, and the utter desolation of the country made any printed maps hard to follow.

We flew into the zone of mountain time, 4 hours behind New York daylight and 8 hours behind Greenwich civil time. So it must have been 11 o'clock in the morning, when, at 17:13, we were headed south-southeast and making fast time, as we tore across the south shore of Quiet Lake. Herds of caribou—or maybe they were some other northern animals—scattered at our approach and scampered into the forests as the hills quaked with our echo.

Down the shelf of the colorful Canadian Rockies we flew. Hardly a word passed between Wiley and me. We were both content to sit still and absorb the vitality generated by the crisp air.

It's a good thing we did this while we could, for soon the gods decided the flight had gone too smoothly. Angry at the light way in which the plane had flung itself over the mountain barrier, they sent old Jupiter Pluvius to plague us. We dipped down to a point where we could follow the map and keep the ground in sight through the sheets of water which screened it from view at high altitudes.

My thoughts as we swung into the wide valley which separates the Rockies from the Coast Range in British Columbia were none too pleasant. I felt that we were going to make a record but instead of feeling exuberant about it, I was asking myself: What of it? Who cares? Is it worth this nerve-wracking dive through the rain, or putting my family through the worry I know they must be having?

The loneliness of that country was beginning to upset my mental equilibrium. I tried to talk a little to Wiley, but his monosyllabic replies failed to divert me. I tried to whistle, but the engine drowned out any amusement.

In that pouring rain we still had the high range of the Rockies to vault. A large black shadow, Mt. Merkle, loomed up on the right. The left vista was nothing but the blackness of a yawning chasm as we thundered through the valley to Hudson Hope.

Good old Wiley! He just sat up there and flew. He flew and I blew—up. We picked up the Finlay River where it crosses the valley.

By this time we were running fairly light. We followed the river to the first waterfall, and then hugged the west slope of the Rocky Range. We could see about 2 miles, but objects were indistinct outlines rather than concrete realities.

All this time I had been tracing our route as we followed it. My pencil was busy reversing the compass readings to conform to the map projection. My instruction to Wiley to turn east at Smoky River Pass was anticipated by him, for the compass was turning back to 98° when I first lifted my head to shout through the tube.

Up, up, and still farther up he took the plane. Climbing turn after turn brought us slowly to the sharp abutment which, to British Columbians, divides East from West.

"It's all downhill from here in, kid," Wiley shouted.

"Give her all she can take and let's get this leg over," I returned.

But the old boy never came down so conservatively in his life. He stretched that descent for more than 50 miles, and when we tore through the rain clouds, the first thing which met our eyes was the Canadian National Railway branch that cuts west from Edmonton to Prince Rupert, British Columbia.

That guide was a godsend, a sort of sop for the rain. We ripped off the miles over the tracks like a crack express, with only the click of the wheels across the rail joints missing. Where the railroad widened into the yards, we picked up a high bluff with the Hotel MacDonald on top.

"Edmonton—all out!" Wiley shouted.

But he reckoned without his host. We turned away from the tracks and went right over the center of town, headed northwest for the airport. We followed the same long street that later was to stand us in such good stead.

"Winnie Mae" banked lazily upon her left side as we hovered over the field.

" 'Not a creature was stirring—not even a "Moth",' " I said.

"Gee, I wish we had this crate mounted on floats," was Wiley's remark, as he sighted the sea of mud.

I thought I would never pronounce "Blagoveshchensk"

again after the hours of gloom we had spent there. But on the way into that field at Edmonton I said it faster than the Russian who gave the town its name. As the wheels touched, I closed my eyes and put my hands on the roof. I lifted my head toward Heaven and murmured, "Ah, God, not Blagoveshchensk!"

I never was so proud of any pilot in my life as I was of Wiley when he slopped that ship through the mire and half taxied, half flew it to the hangar apron.

Even though the drenching rain had been coming down steadily for hours, there was a big crowd waiting there to greet us. When "Winnie Mae's" wheels came to a stop, they broke through the police lines and crowded toward us. We stayed in the ship until they were brought under control, but when we finally got out we ran into the same ordeal we had experienced in Berlin—photographers, radio announcers, and reporters seemingly without number, all trying to get our attention at the same time.

Wiley was so tired, so disheartened, and so apprehensive on account of the mud-soaked condition of the field that he had two or three bitter remarks under his breath, which fortunately were unnoticed by the hospitable Canadians. In the turmoil somebody held a microphone up in front of him, but all he could think of saying was that he was tired of sitting down.

As for myself, it was such a pleasure to be back where we didn't have to spend an hour or more trying to find an interpreter or attempting to make our wants known by the sign language, that even the quagmire that the rain had made of the flying field didn't dishearten me. I felt sure that, somehow or other, Wiley and the "Winnie Mae" would manage to get off, even if we had to take an acre or two of wheat soil with us.

The customs and immigration officials went through the formalities of passing us through very quickly and efficiently. We were shown into one of the offices at the airport, where we received the official welcome of Major James M. Douglas, representing the city of Edmonton, and the Honorable Vernor Smith, acting premier of Alberta. Both of them said a lot of nice things about us, but I'm afraid we were so tired and so perplexed about how we were going to get off, that we were scarcely more than superficially polite.

For an hour or so we stayed at the airport, trying to make up our minds how to meet the problem. We had intended to refuel and take off at once, but that was simply out of the question. In fact, Wiley and I were both afraid that even though the rain stopped, the field wouldn't dry out enough by morning to give "Winnie Mae" a footing from which she could get into the air.

Several Canadian air-mail pilots were in the group which had crowded into the office, and one of them made the suggestion that saved the day. He pointed out that Portage Avenue ran straight for 2 miles from the flying field to town. Its paved surface and lack of bordering obstacles, which would set up cross air currents, made it an almost ideal runway, and it was plenty wide enough.

This sounded good to us, and when our hosts saw how relieved we were at finding a way out of the situation, they put emergency crews to work taking down the electric-light wires along that street.

They escorted us to the hotel, where we found a flood of mail and telegrams waiting for us.

Of course, sleep was our main idea, but we had some trouble because of the number of telephone calls from newspapers and other sources, from places as far away as New York. But our hosts shielded us vigilantly from most of the disturbances and made it possible for us to turn in early, now able to rest with our minds freed from the fear that we would not be able to get away in the morning.

14

JULY 1

EDMONTON TO NEW YORK

(POST)

WHEN WE ARRIVED AT THE EDMONTON AIRPORT EARLY THE NEXT morning, we found that the town had turned out in a body to see us go. All the flying mud of the night before had been washed away from "Winnie Mae," and she appeared dressed up in her finest white. Gatty said she reminded him of a little girl all ready to be flower girl at a wedding.

As we warmed up the engine, the rain stopped. I had told Harold to stay away from that propeller and let the mechanics at the field do all the work. The ship was towed out to the sidewalk, and a pair of "mounties" dashed up and down the street in an automobile, clearing away all traffic.

At 3:30 A.M. by the local time and 6:30 by New York daylight (the time on my watch which I had kept for the past 8 days so that I could time our entrance into Roosevelt Field), I taxied out to the unused street-car tracks and faced the nose toward the hotel, 2 miles away, at which we had stayed.

People crowded uncomfortably close to the ship, and I

am afraid we seemed impolite to them. Dirt, mud, and spray flew all around while I "revved" the motor up one last time before letting go the brakes. We were to bobble off headed straight for the center of town, and I didn't want to take any chances of being let down among the corners of the buildings.

3:38:45 A.M. and I let the Wasp have her head. Like a darky pursued by a ghost, the ship hurtled down that street. Curbstones and electric-light poles clipped by the wing tips so fast that I was just a little scared myself. The wind was slightly across our path, and if one wing had ever dropped, it would have been just too bad.

I'm sure neither Harold nor I ever went or ever will go down a street so fast again. I got a new idea of the ground speed of the "Winnie Mae." Loafing along an airport runway, with nothing upright nearer the plane than 100 yards or so, reduces the sensation of high speeds, but I know now what 75 miles an hour feels like!

Within 15 seconds the outlying houses of town had dropped under the nose. By the time we reached the first turn in the street, we had a good 500 feet, and as I came over the Hotel MacDonald, where our late *maitre d'hotel* was out on the roof with his whole army of bellhops in array to salute us going by, the ground dropped away fast, and we turned over the high bluff which the hotel tops.

In a few minutes we caught up with the rain. We didn't mind that, though; we were glad that it was going our way. The wind was on our tail. It was one of the few times that I had found the wind blowing any way but against the nose of the ship without having had to wait for it to turn around.

"Set your course at 83½°," came Harold's instruction.

"What do you mean 'one half'?" I returned.

On an aërial compass it is hard enough to read within one degree, but Harold never will get over the habits he developed when he used one of those ship compasses, which can be made as big as the whole cockpit of the "Winnie Mae."

I pointed her at 83° and throttled back to cruising. We were making tracks fast. We didn't have to do much navigating as the country in Alberta and Saskatchewan is so regularly divided by the section lines, which cut it up into square miles, that once you start across the lines at a certain angle, you can keep cutting them at the same angle. A pilot can throw away his compass up there and still hit his destination right on the nose of the ship.

We picked up North Battleford, Saskatchewan, in about an hour. Then Saskatoon, an old-fashioned prairie town. Yorkton swung by about 2 miles to the right. The weather began clearing as we started across Manitoba for the Great Lakes.

It was with more than a little thrill that I nosed out over the shore of Lake Superior. In 26 minutes we barged into the good old U. S. A., just north from Bessemer Junction, Michigan, and for the next few minutes that northern half of Michigan went under our nose almost too fast to suit me. Gogebic Lake, Iron River, and the northeastern tip of Wisconsin went by, then we crossed Green Bay and flew out over Lake Michigan.

As we ran into the main part of Michigan and passed over Flint, Pontiac, and Detroit, I shouted back to Gatty, "How does this look to you?"

"Didn't see any country I liked better on the whole trip," he said. "I make it 5 o'clock by New York time, so we'd better hurry if we want to get there in daylight."

I opened up and ripped the air apart as we crossed Lake Erie. I would hurry now and land, because in a few hours I was going to get a "beeg sleep like the bahr in weenter," to quote an old French Canadian I once knew.

It was 5:15 by our watches on New York daylight time

when we rolled in at the Municipal Airport in Cleveland. There was a big crowd out and so much excitement that I completely lost my course on the ground there. Photographers, a fellow named Shanahan who sketched both of us, radio announcers, reporters and sporting celebrities who were there for the Stribling-Schmeling fight, all took us by storm.

I was getting used to being mobbed by this time, but Gatty was developing a desire for seclusion. He would duck as soon as a group started toward us, and some one would have to drag him back. He lost the pocket from his coat that way at the Cleveland airport.

Up we went after half an hour, with a new load of gas. The rest of the flight, from Cleveland to New York, was uneventful. It has been made by the mail flyers more than 10 times every 24 hours for the past year and a half. The air-mail revolving beacons were already turned on when we crossed over Bellefonte, Pennsylvania, and the rocky ridges of the Alleghenies.

Then came the biggest thrill of my life and of Harold's, too, for that matter—the New York sky line. What a sight! We had gone all the way around the world for a glimpse of it from the west!

The first of a lot of planes from Roosevelt Field to pick us up was Martin Jensen's old Breeze monoplane, now flown by Hal MacMahon and fitted out for aërial photography. The old ship may have flown to Hawaii, but it couldn't stay with "Winnie Mae" for speed, and we left it in the lurch in no time.

Brooklyn, Jamaica, and Mineola all tumbled into a disorderly jumble before my tired eye. Then I shot over the hangars which had dropped off the nose less than 9 days before. I was about to cut and land on the same spot from which we had taken off, when I saw the crowd waiting at the other field. The air was filled with planes, and I wanted to get down before we spoiled the whole trip by running into one of them. They were filled with photographers, and their pilots brought them pretty close to us so that we could be "shot."

"Make a turn and give them a chance," Harold called. "I would rather let them have it up here than be made to walk the plank afterward and be photographed by the hour."

I still smile when I remember how easy he thought it was going to be to satisfy photographers. I have yet to learn what they do with all the pictures they take.

Even though it added a minute or more to the record, I made a wide turn for the cameramen. Then, against the southeast wind, I came in for my final landing. I had to come in high over the hangars and the crowd, for I was tired and didn't want to take any chances. I slipped "Winnie Mae" down on her left wing, pulled her out with the tail low and the motor pulling slightly, and touched on the hard-surfaced runway.

As I taxied back, flares and flash lights blinded me, and as I reached the edge of the running crowd I quit. I was afraid somebody might walk into the whirling propeller, so I cut the switch before the ship was off the runway.

"Well, here we are, kid," I called back to Harold.

But Harold was already out of the ship. He had ducked around the tail. They chased him back in again so that he could be photographed. As he put on his helmet once more, I called through the ear phone:

"Murderers and around-the-world flyers all have to get 'mugged' in their working clothes."

When we got out, pandemonium broke loose. The police were helpless to protect us.

Through the whirligig of crowds, flash lights, reporters, broadcasts, and whatnot which followed, just one thing stands out in my memory. Walter D. Ward, New York timer of the National Aëronautic Association, who checked us out and in at Roosevelt Field, computed and announced our official time—8 days, 15 hours, 51 minutes.

"Gee," said Harold, "let them shoot a while at that!"

All I know of the next few days is a muddle. The rest I planned never came. We were wined and dined until the very sight of food made me shudder.

I even remember wishing that I had cracked up on the last landing. Then, at least, I would have had a nice reclining ride in an ambulance to some quiet hospital, where my dream of sleep would have been realized.

People were enthusiastic and solicitous. But how we would have appreciated a 3-day postponement of the celebrations which followed our trip around the world in 8 days! Even Mr. Hall, Mrs. Gatty, and Mrs. Post, who needed sleep almost as much as we did, were pressed into service for the next few days as "emergency police" to help the big sergeant who stood guard outside our suite in the Ritz Carlton Hotel.

Parading through the ticker tape of lower Broadway is an experience that I would not have missed, however, and we found Mayor James J. Walker an ideal host.

But the sweetest moment came when we boarded William H. Todd's steam yacht 2 days later. I took possession of the best spot on deck and in a few minutes was "A.W.O.L." for 4 or 5 solid hours.

In our flight around the world, I had satisfied my life's ambition. But it was Harold who was the guiding hand of the "Winnie Mae." All I did was to follow his instructions in steering, and to keep the ship from spinning out of the thick "pea soup," of which we encountered so much in our trip Around the World in Eight Days.

Part Three

Autobiographical

15

POST TRACES HIS EARLY HISTORY

(POST)

HOW DID I HAPPEN TO GET TO BE AN AVIATOR, AND A PILOT FOR Mr. Hall? I would rather tell the life story of Harold Gatty than my own, but I'll take a chance:

I was born—they told me so before I was three years old—in my father's house on a farm near Grand Saline, Texas, on the night of November 22, 1899. My father, William Francis Post, was of Scotch descent, and the owner of a 160-acre (quarter-section) farm. My mother was Mae Quinlan before her marriage; I hardly need say what her nationality was.

I was the fourth son, and when I was three years old, my only sister, Mary, was born and soon became the pet of the family. That left me pretty much alone, both in the house and on the farm. Nobody seemed to care much what I did as long as I took care of the few simple chores I was supposed to do each day.

Before I was old enough to go to school, I remember that the chief topic of conversation at the dinner table was the discovery of oil in Indian Territory. Many of the farmers who lived near Grand Saline were picking up stakes and migrating into the reservation, sinking life savings into leases near oil-producing areas.

In the midst of the wave of farm prosperity which came as mushroom cities sprang up near the Texas line in Oklahoma, we moved to Abilene, Texas. The owner of a full half section (320 acres) sold out cheap to my father, so he could go leaseholding in the oil country.

The acquisition of a larger farm necessitated more machinery, and I shall always remember my first sight of a new harvester. It marked my first interest in mechanics. My father and three older brothers pored over the instruction books and scurried around the machine, squirting oil on the various bearings. I still remember the clicking sounds from the copper squirt can. They said I was always under their feet and in the way, and I know I was continually being shooed away from the knives.

The harvester—even after a month of use, when its newness and gaudy paint were gone—continued to attract me, and I soon learned the function of every part.

It was in Abilene that I got my first taste of school. I didn't like it, and my reaction was obvious both to the teacher and to my parents. Texas is a nice place if you are outdoors, but inside a schoolhouse, under the thumb of a strict taskmaster, if you're six years old and having trouble with geography, it gets hot and dull. They had no kindergarten or any such frills in that rural school.

About this time I was left more than ever to myself on the farm. We had a new baby again, a boy. We named him—my mother did, I mean—Byron, and nowadays he's a bit of an amateur pilot himself. He kept my mother too busy for her to keep tabs on me. My sister played with him like a doll, and she, too, quite forgot about me.

So I had a fine chance to inspect the harvester and other machines. In the back of my mind I could see a lot of things wrong with them. Maybe, even yet, I'll stop in some day where they are made and show the people who make them my ideas of how to improve them.

Well, to get on with my story, I was just the kind of a lad to thrive in Texas—or Oklahoma, where the family moved, near Chickasha, in 1907. Land cost more the nearer you got to the oil country, so we had only a quarter section again. By this time I was saddled with Mary on the way to school. Joe, the brother three years my elder, made me take care of her.

I was always being compared with Jim, my eldest brother, who was eight years older than I and the star student of the family. The next oldest was Arthur.

When Gordon was born, after the family had moved to a half-section farm again, in Maysville, I thought I was old enough to decide matters for myself. The first thing I decided was that my talents were wasted in school; that geography didn't mix well with me. So I relaxed and gave my academic career little thought after I reached my eleventh year.

I proved my independence by starting to earn money in the neighborhood fixing things. By the time I was thirteen, I had saved enough to buy the first bicycle in the district. Gradually I widened the area in which I was the main "tinker." Repairing sewing machines, sharpening reaper knives, and fixing other articles of household and farm machinery came easy to me and brought in a little ready cash. Well, that gives you an idea of how things were when I was small.

It was in the following year, 1913, that I got my first real inspiration. The county fair was being held in Lawton, some fifty miles from our farm, and the whole community was talking about the "aëroplane ascent" that was going to be part of the daily show. I tried to hornswoggle my father into letting me go. After I did some extra work and promised to pay two admissions out of my savings, he finally said yes, and sent my brother Jim along with me in the horse and buggy.

I remember we started out early in the evening and it took all night to get there. Along toward morning we trotted over a rise in the prairie and came within sight of the fairgrounds at Lawton. The nag pricked up his ears and quickened his lagging steps.

Jim and I found a place to hitch the horse. We pulled off his harness and then started out to see the show. We were excited enough to begin with, but that excitement was nothing compared to what mine was before the day was over.

We looked over the prize cows and the exhibits of maize and cotton and other products of the field, and Jim took in everything. I wanted to get through with nature study and have a look at the machinery. New plows and tractors and reapers, gay in bright reds and blues, were bunched together across the midway. So I left Jim and started over— but I never got there. I don't know to this day what kind of harvesters and planters were on display.

Standing out in the open field that served as the midway inside the race track, was a queer-looking contraption. I stopped and looked. There before my astonished vision was an "aëroplane"—that's what they called them in this country then. That agricultural fair changed itself into an air meet for me then and there. The machine was an old Curtiss pusher. I promptly spent the morning with it. To this day I have never seen a bit of machinery for land, sea, or sky that has taken my breath away as did that old pusher. Yet I have to smile now when I think of how wonderful it seemed to me then.

Shortly after lunch Art Smith, the ship's pilot, appeared and became the first real hero I had ever seen. I nearly got into trouble hanging around the plane. The constable, special policeman, or whatever he was, chased me away about ten times, but I succeeded in getting close enough to Smith (and the machine) to hear him talk.

When it began to grow dark, I sneaked back to where the plane was. I paced off its length and width and measured the height in "hands," just as I had seen my father and brothers step off horses in trades.

I was sitting in the rickety seat—they didn't have enclosed cockpits then—when my brother found me. I had promised to meet him at the spot where we had left the horse, and he'd been looking for me nearly two hours. I had forgotten to feed and water the poor animal, too, and it had been a hot day. But Jim had taken care of him, so I got away with that.

I saw the first automobile (we put the accent on the second *o*) of my life at that fair, too, but it seemed unimportant beside the aëorplane. I had seen plenty of pictures of automobiles in the advertisements of the farm magazines we used to take, so I was able even to tell the make. "Gas buggies," as we used to call them, were pretty much hated by the farmers because they scared the horses so

Secretly, I had been forming the Wiley Post Institute for Aëronautical Research there at the country fair. In fact, I was so engrossed in thought that, when I took my turn at driving the horse on that long night drive home I was imagining myself doing the 30-miles-an-hour air speed of the Curtiss pusher. My brother woke up a couple of times and had to give me a little "dual instruction" in horse-and-buggy flying.

In that quiet country—it's not so quiet any more—the only roads were wagon lanes where the sand was deep. An automobile caught up with us on the road home, and our tired horse nearly ran away with us. If he had been fresh, he might have succeeded, but dragging even the light buggy through what was, by that time, about eighty miles of sand was too much for him. Finally he just stood still and shivered with fear. With much rattling and tooting, the automobile finally got by us and nearly choked us to death with the heavy cloud of gritty dust it threw up.

We just couldn't seem to lose that car, though. In a few miles we came on it again, stuck in the sand. The owner offered us a dollar if we would lend him our horse, but the animal wouldn't go near the dusty machine.

Chickasha was pretty near home, however, and I made a deal with the driver that I would bring back help from there if he would give me the dollar and take me home after he got started again. About five miles farther on I got a team that was used to working near engines. The owner, Joe Crawford, had a sawmill that he used to cart around to cut wood at various places. With two of the three men pushing and the other one driving, while I coaxed hard at the team, we finally got the automobile up on firm ground. I rode one of the horses back for the five miles and then started on toward home in the gas buggy—my first automobile ride.

I'll never forget how mad Jim was that day. We passed him about a mile from the house. The road was hard and wide there, and the nag took his head out from between his forelegs and galloped through a grove into a field. Jim looked funny when he got out; he shook his fist after us, and I, with entire lack of sympathy, laughed with the others in the machine. The machine age was coming; I knew it. When I arrived at the farm ahead of Jim, the family gathered around while the three strangers put water into the radiator. They had left Lawton much later than we had, and their trip seemed greater to me then than our recent flight around the world does now.

Those two days had a great effect on my life. My interest in mechanical things doubled, and in the next two and a half years I helped equip the farm with a gasoline engine.

We used it to pump water, and by fixing up a series of belts, I made it run a corn sheller, a grindstone, a buzz saw, and a lot of other things which made the work around the farm easier.

In 1916 I decided that Oklahoma needed a good trained mechanic. Things were going well at home, except that I still disliked school. I went to Kansas City to take up a course in the Sweeney Auto School, one of the first of its kind. I spent seven months there and came out (if I may say so) a good chauffeur and mechanic. I still had a hankering for further knowledge along engineering lines.

Underneath it all, however, Art Smith and his flying contraption were a continual source of speculation to me. No matter what I did or where I worked, I looked at each new piece of machinery with the underlying thought that its principle might be applied to aviation. I read a great deal, studied mathematics by myself, and experimented a bit with chemistry.

My first real job was back in Lawton. I worked for the Chickasha & Lawton Construction Company. The United States was in the War then, and the Government was building an airport at Fort Sill.

Although the airport was named Post Field, I had nothing to do with it beyond a bit of driving and grading. After six months or more of work there, in the summer of 1917, I left to join the Students' Army Training Camp at Norman, where we used the University of Oklahoma buildings. I studied radio, and my previous work in mathematics and chemistry stood me in good stead.

Section A of the Radio School was graduated and sent with the troops to France. My three older brothers were already on the sea on their way to the battlefields. But my section, B, was dismissed as soon as the Armistice was signed in 1918, and I was once again left to my own resources. However, I was better equipped than ever before.

I had learned to do engineering work. I could do a bit of mechanical drafting, and my mind had been trained to cope with scientific details.

The first problem for all of us, after the War, was to get a job. I finally located at Walters, Oklahoma, in the south-central part of the state, where a new oil field was opening up. Because of my bent for mechanics, I soon learned to be a "roughneck" on a drilling rig and did all the odd tasks about the place. A roughneck in that part of the business is a general handy man. We got $7 a day, but the work was hard and dirty. Sometimes I fed boilers, sometimes I had to climb the derrick to thread pulleys, and at other times I drove the cars.

I graduated from roughneck on a drilling rig to tool-dresser at $11 a day, and within a short time was getting to the stage where I might claim to be a full-fledged driller. Drillers got $25 a day. Uppermost in my mind at that time was the need of saving money, and the good pay kept me going. 'Way out there in the oil fields there was nothing to spend money on, and I soon found that I had quite a stake.

The gambling fever of the oil fields hit me hard. My first stake went when I put it all into a wildcat scheme. I went back to work as a driller and soon saved another stake. But that went, too, when I tried to get rich quick by leasing ground near a wildcat well which petered out.

Just about this time, the summer of 1919, a great wave of barnstorming airplane pilots began to visit the towns in Oklahoma, with their ancient planes held together with baling wire. Seeing one, I suddenly got the notion that I would like to ride in the air. A Captain Zimmerman was in Walters, and I paid him $25 to take me up and put me through all the maneuvers he knew.

Frankly, that first flight was a disappointment to me. I expected a much bigger thrill than I got for my money. The plane, as I look back on it, was incapable of doing any startling stunt, and while I got a little squeamish in the air, I didn't feel that aviators necessarily had those supernatural powers I had been reading about in magazine stories.

So I went back to the rig and resumed my duties as a driller. Seesawing between gambling the stake on a hole of my own and working for other drillers, I somehow was able to get through the next four and a half years.

Twice I thought I had made the grade by leasing ground supposed to cover oil, but both times I was wrong. Then I got disgusted with the oil business. The price of oil went so low that none of the operators was anxious to drill.

One day, when I was on a drilling job near Holdenville in the eastern section of the state, I saw a plane overhead. The old urge to fly came over me, and straightway I embarked on my aviation career. I quit the oil business once and for all, I thought, and headed for a little town of Wewoka, ten miles or so west from Holdenville, where a flying circus was advertised.

I found the field all right, but the three men who ran the flying circus did not seem to want any addition to their troupe. But since I knew them, I finally persuaded them to listen to me. They had two planes, both old Canucks. The ships were rather worn and battered, but were great improvements over the JN-4's after which they were patterned.

Pete Lewis was the exhibition parachute jumper of the circus. He had made three jumps the week I showed up at the field, and on the last one he had been slightly hurt in a landing. I volunteered to make the jump for him the next day, and the others in the troupe agreed to let me do it.

The parachutes used in those days were of the Hardin exhibition type. The 'chute was packed in a bag which was tied to one of the interplane struts in the bay of the right wing. There was a little cord attached to the release which let the 'chute out of the bag, and a rope, strong enough to hold the end of the canopy but intended to break with a man's weight, pulled the 'chute open in the wind. They were queer contraptions, those old-type parachutes, but I had good instruction from Lewis before I went up.

When it was time for the performances the next day, I buckled on the harness and got into the plane with Berl Tibbs, the chief pilot of the circus. I think he figured I was just framing him for a free airplane ride, because he threatened to get even if I got scared and called off my jump after we once got in the air. I don't know what convinced him, but he finally wobbled down the runway and took off.

We got up about 2,000 feet above the usual rural-airport Sunday crowd when he cut his throttle and called to me, "O.K. Get ready."

I was somewhat taken aback, now that the time had arrived. I hesitated not so much through fear as through ignorance. I seemed to have forgotten all the things Lewis had told me to do.

I looked back helplessly at Tibbs, but got only a glare in return. Suddenly I recovered myself and threw one leg out over the wing. Tibbs cut his throttle again, so that the slipstream of the propeller wouldn't blow me off. I grabbed the cabane strut which held the upper wing in the center to the fuselage, and slowly made my way to the interplane set. Hanging tight to the strut with one hand, and buckling the harness to the snap rings of the parachute, I dropped on my knees.

The motor came on full again as Tibbs turned the ship to get into position so that I would land near the airport. By this time I was beyond the immediate area of the slipstream, and the wind hardly increased at all. I looked toward the pilot again, and he pointed off to the right as he made a turn. At last he leveled off.

"Let's go!" he shouted.

I let go the strut and backed off the wing. I swung help-lessly out underneath. For several seconds I hung there before I remembered what to do next. Then I found the release string and pulled with all my might.

Suddenly all motion stopped. I seemed to be floating in the air. The plane was gone. I did not have the sensation of falling I had anticipated. With a sharp jerk, the para-chute opened. I looked up and saw it spread out above me. I grabbed the old "shroud ring," made from the steer-ing wheel of an automobile. (Originally the idea of this shroud ring was to steer the parachute to a landing, but it didn't work. They left it on the lines, however, because it helped make the 'chute more comfortable, and gave the jumper something stable to hang on to.)

While still hanging tight to the ring, I first felt the sinking sensation. I swallowed hard and for the first time looked straight down. That was one of the biggest thrills of my life. The people below looked like so many ants and the fields looked like brown or green carpets. I tried to get a line on where I was going to hit, but I couldn't. Then I heard the plane. Looking up again, I saw Tibbs circling above in a tight turn.

Gradually things took shape. I guess it didn't take more than two minutes for the drop, but to me it seemed like a couple of hours. I never saw so much which stuck in my memory in so short a time.

I watched the trees get bigger. At first they were just trees, but soon I was able to tell what kind they were. Then the fences came up at me. There were no telephone wires to worry about. Gradually I drifted earthward, and I saw that I was going beyond the airport. I skimmed over the edge of a big sycamore which bordered a grove beyond the flying field, and lost the last few feet of altitude slowly because of the cool eddies of air from the damp, plowed meadow beyond.

There was only a slight bump as I flexed my knees for the landing. My feet stuck in the furrows. The wind took the parachute ahead of me, and I fell on my face. I had been told to face into the breeze and run as soon as I hit. The first step was as far as I got.

In spite of making my first landing "on my nose," I had a great sense of satisfaction. Even if I weren't going to get paid for the stunt, I felt that I was at last part of the aviation industry. I had made successfully the first full-scale test of the Wiley Post Institute for Aëronautical Research.

That was my beginning. The next week I did another jump. This time I got $50 for it. Soon I became a regular performer in the flying circus and was attached to the second plane, which was usually flown by a student of Tibbs, a young fellow named "Tip" Schier.

My price for jumping was soon raised to $100, and Tibbs' outfit wouldn't pay it. So I resolved to go into business on my own.

"Town boosting" was the order of the day in Oklahoma communities in 1924, so it was easy for me to interest chambers of commerce and Rotary Club members in staging a parachute jump on Sundays. Frequently I got as high as $200 for a single jump. I had to pay a pilot and also plane hire out of my price, but that seldom came to more than $25. I didn't care how good or how poor a flyer the pilot was, and always took the plane which was nearest the town in which I was to perform. I was an actor, my own manager, and bookkeeper, in addition to holding my place at the head of the Wiley Post Institute.

In the first two years of that work I got in a few hours of dual flying while working with pilots that I knew. I got most of my early lessons from a pilot named Sam Bartel.

Perhaps the most exciting time I had in that period of my life was my invasion of Maysville, where my folks lived. I came almost at the start of my independent career. Up to that time I had been using assumed names. But I thought I could start using my own name by making good as the "hometown boy," so I called on the Maysville Chamber of Commerce one Monday afternoon and told them I would stage a jump the following Sunday. Because it was my own town and I knew the men so well, I gave them reduced rates, $75 for the day.

I made arrangements to hire a young pilot with an old Standard biplane from Pauls Valley, about ten miles away. Then I went home to my parents. My parachute and equipment were under my arm, and I took the family breath away when I told them I was a parachute jumper and was going to perform in town on Sunday. My father tried to dissuade me, but my mother was so glad to see me that it didn't take much persuasion to induce her to get him to stop arguing with me.

Well, the circus was advertised all over town. I noticed that my father refused to talk about it. But the whole town assured me it was a great stunt and promised to be out in the open meadow where Virgil Turnbull, my pilot from Pauls Valley, was to pick me up. Virgil had had only about 150 hours in the air at that time, so I drove over to see him about landing in the short field.

When I got home, I looked for my parachute to see that it was properly packed. It was gone! I searched all over the place for it. I looked in all the closets, the attic, the outbuildings, and finally I asked the neighbors. But from that day to this, I have never seen that parachute. My father was not much disturbed about its disappearance. That made me suspicious. Not that I would accuse him of taking it—of course, he didn't want to jump—but—!

That was the worst setback my aviation career ever suffered. I had to go to the men who were getting the crowd out and apologize. I guess a lot of them thought I had just been bluffing them. I promised to get another 'chute and be ready by the next week.

I went by train to Oklahoma City and borrowed a parachute. But I didn't take it home. No, sir! I had promised the officials that nothing short of a tornado would stop the show the next Sunday. I went straight to Pauls Valley with it and waited there for the start, telegraphing to Maysville that I would be over the town at 3 o'clock sharp.

So Virgil wound up the OX motor in the Standard, and after a big Sunday dinner at his house, we started off. We circled over Maysville a couple of times and gave the folks a little sideshow while the crowd was gathering—a few loops and one slow roll. The rest was just climbing and diving. I spent my time watching the gyrations of the dual-stick socket and the motions of the rudder pedals as the plane dived, zoomed, and rolled about. I still had visions of getting enough money together to buy a plane and become a pilot.

The jump went off in good style, and I landed almost exactly on the spot agreed on by the committee. By that time I had learned to gauge my stepping-off place so that I could pick my landings. When I got home, even my father expressed his admiration. I was a hero (of a sort) in my own home town!

Things went on like that for nearly two years. Gradually the barnstorming business grew worse, however, and prices declined. People were getting so used to airplanes that they hardly even looked up at them any more. Planes were for sale all over the country, and $150 would buy one. But most of them were man-killers, so I left them alone.

By that time I had had about four hours of dual flying and felt ready to solo. I forgot one thing. I had taken off in a plane many times, but I could count on my fingers the number of times I had landed.

In spite of this I went to Sam Bartel. Sam made me put up $200 as security that I wouldn't ruin his $150 Canuck, but I had a lot of confidence in myself. As I look back on it now, I realize that I was not ready to solo then, but I did it.

That flight was a great sensation for me, too. I got into the plane, leaving the parachute on the ground. I wound up the OX and tested it out as if I had been doing it all my life.

It wasn't until after I had wobbled down the rough ground and cleared the fence that I realized I was all alone in the plane. For the first time in my life I was almost frightened. There was nothing I could do but go on climbing. I went up to where I felt comfortable and flew around for nearly half an hour before I felt sufficiently sure of myself to attempt a landing. Then I cut the gun.

I stuck the nose over and started down. I forgot to clear the motor out occasionally, and the thing coughed and sputtered. Then I got really scared. Was my first solo to end in a forced landing? I shot the throttle forward. With some hesitation the engine caught again, but I neglected to pull the nose up soon enough. Almost immediately I was diving toward the ground so fast that a third spasm of fright paralyzed my mind. I discovered later that I barely missed a tree with my right wing before I pulled the ship up again and made another flat turn of the field.

That time I came in for a landing. I slipped in over the fence a little high, and maybe leveled off a bit too soon, but I succeeded in getting down without breaking anything. I made one more flight alone and called it a day. Sam gave me back my deposit in full and didn't charge me for the flights. He said he thought I was showing off on that first try!

16

"WINNIE MAE" GOES RECORD-HUNTING

(POST)

ABOUT THIS TIME IN MY CAREER, WHILE WAITING ON A FIELD TO go up and make a jump, I saw an old JN-4 crash and burn. I rushed with the crowd to try and get the poor devils out of it, but it was all over before we could do anything. I knew both the men well. I had flown several times with the pilot, and the accident might just as well have happened when I was along.

It was one of those crashes in which a split second or a fraction of a mile an hour in speed meant safety or disaster. Those old planes flew, glided, took off, or landed all within a range of a scant 10 miles an hour.

The reaction of the audience to the crash was unbelievable. I shall never forget the smug satisfaction apparent in that crowd. At first I refused to believe it. Then, when I realized the truth, I spent the most miserable two weeks of my existence.

To think that the spectators of airplane maneuvers were just a bloodthirsty mob that enjoyed watching men get killed was just a little more than I could stand. I got mad.

I would show them. I was so impressed by the whole affair that it revolutionized my technique in staging future exhibitions.

I started doing delayed drops. I left the plane with two parachutes. I waited to pull the rip cord. While I was tearing down, I could feel the exultance of the crowd. My grin on landing, after giving the side lines a thrill, was not one of pleasure. It was one of victory. I had fooled them!

I was studying crowd psychology. My desire to thwart the spectator's hope of witnessing my untimely end was so strong that at times I grew so reckless as to scare myself.

Later, I was glad to find that I had been a little too severe a critic. I realized that part of the fault had been with the men who staged the shows. Their lack of coöperation and of appeciation of one another had promoted a decidedly unfriendly spirit of rivalry.

The tough going in the business had much to do with that. Private contractors had taken over the operation of the air-mail lines from the Government. The air lines had absorbed most of the more experienced pilots, and had left the barnstorming field to the youthful graduates of commercial flying schools. These youngsters were intent only on supporting themselves until they had had enough time in the air to get on as mail pilots. Some of them would even fly for the price of the gas and oil.

So things went from bad to worse. I knew that I couldn't hope to go on unless I, too, joined the rank of flyers whose sole object was to build up time. But to do it I needed an airplane. And money was scarce.

Just about that time, December, 1925, the new oil field at Seminole was opening up. Much as I disliked to admit defeat, I went back to drilling. I resolved to quit as soon as I had enough money to buy a good airplane.

But another setback came. My first day on the drilling rig a roughneck was driving a bolt through the derrick. I was directing the work. The sledge came down hard on the head of the iron bolt. Under the terrific blows of the hammer a chip flew off and struck my left eyeball before I had a chance to close the lid. Infection set in, and the doctors found it necessary to take my eye out.

But I didn't stay discouraged. In the two months I spent with an uncle in the hills of southwest Texas, recuperating, I had plenty of time to think. The sight of my right eye was gradually returning to normal and I practiced gauging depth on hills and trees. I would look at a tree and try to guess its distance from me. Then I would step off the distance. I did the same with hills, and timed my 4-mile-an-hour gait as a check on my judgment. At first, my mental calculations were far off, but by the end of the two months I was a better judge of distance than I had ever been. It seemed funny, though, to practice looking.

The Workmen's Compensation Law awarded me $1,800 for the eye, and after paying out my expenses I still had more than $1,200 left. My intention to get the cost of an airplane was realized—at the expense of an eye!

I was in fine shape physically. Those two months in the Davis Mountains had done me good. My uncle and I had hunted and bagged some quail and a couple of deer, and had rid the country of a lot of coyotes.

I finally found a Canuck with an OX-5 motor which suited my purpose. It had been in a slight crash, and the two young fellows who owned it couldn't afford to repair it. I gave them $240 for the plane and spent $300 having it rebuilt throughout.

I took the ship, and got one of the original owners to fly me back to Holdenville. Then I got Sam Bartel to give me about two hours' dual on it and practiced about three hours more around his field.

I started out on my own with the plane shortly before Lindbergh's transatlantic flight. I remember being in Ardmore, Oklahoma, when all the excitement was going on at Roosevelt Field, Long Island, in April and May of 1927. Through hard work I had built up what was practically a monopoly in flying in the rough country of southeast Oklahoma, southern Arkansas, and northeast Texas. The lower end of the Ozarks joins the Kiamichi Range there, and flying is bad. Lots of local fog, bad currents of air, and plenty of scrub timber make emergency landings almost impossible. I hired out to flying circuses on Sundays and to oilmen who wanted to get to new leaseholdings quickly. Besides, I picked up a few dollars instructing occasionally.

At Sweetwater, Texas, where I spend a lot of Sundays hopping passengers on commission, I got my first thrill aside from aviation. Her name was Mae Laine, and she is now Mrs. Post. She was seventeen and an ardent air enthusiast. My business suffered a little because several times I refused fares which would keep me too far from Sweetwater over the week-end.

So on June 27, 1927, after the business of the day was over, the soon-to-be Mrs. Post and I piled into the ship. She had a small bag with her, and I had a license in my pocket. Her father, Dave Laine, a rancher on a small scale, was not favorably disposed to our marriage, so we decided to take the matter into our own hands. Together we fled the town.

My $240 airplane had been in the air more than 800 hours since I had bought it, and had never let me down. It had been top-overhauled several times, and I thought it would hold out that evening.

But we both were a little nervous, I guess, and my old companion, the plane, must have got sympathetic tremors. Over Graham, Oklahoma, the rotor in the magneto distributor suddenly ground itself to powder, and the gallant OX gasped and then quit.

It was a bad time for my first forced landing. I looked

over at a cornfield where the fodder was set in rows, cut and shocked. I headed for it, and we smacked down on the rough ground. Bouncing along between two wind-rows, the wing tips overrode the tops of the shocks and lifted the plane a little, but fortunately the good old ship was strong enough to stand it.

After installing a new rotor, by moving the corn shocks back we got off again. In the meantime, we had taken time off to get the local parson to marry us. After that we had no fear of pursuit.

Mrs. Post's interest in flying kept her with me all the time until I sold the Canuck in order to go to work for Mr. Hall, who was to play so great a part in my later life.

It was in 1928, when I first gave up the barnstorming business because it could no longer provide a living now that there were two instead of one, that I visited a friend of mine, Powell Briscoe, who introduced me to Mr. Hall.

On hearing that I was a flyer, the oilman became interested in me. I learned that he had missed out on some leasing deal because he hadn't been able to get to the leaseholder's house fast enough. In the course of the conversation I suggested to Mr. Hall that if he were to own an airplane, he could always get to places faster than anyone else.

Evidently the loss of the lease had already sold him that idea, so he offered me a place as his pilot and assistant. I helped him buy his first airplane, which was the best I had flown up to that time. It was a three-passenger Travelair. Mrs. Post and I took an apartment in Oklahoma City, and we made that our center of operations.

There is nothing of especial interest to relate about that year of flying the Travelair. Mr. Hall would give me my orders, and I would carry him, or anyone else he wanted carried, to any point in Oklahoma, Arkansas, Kansas, or Texas. I knew the country so well from my years of barnstorming that I didn't even need maps. Sometimes I took a chance in overloading the plane with four or five passengers. We didn't have any license for it or for me, so it didn't matter as long as we got down all right.

I would like to tell something about Mr. Hall, because it was due to him that the around-the-world flight became possible. F. C. Hall is a very unusual man. Although he is a born gambler, he has about the best judgment of any man I have ever known. For many years he worked in a drug store in Texas. He was one of the first to get into the swing of oil-leasing. Mr. Hall has a record to date of having drilled more than 300 wells, and he has drilled only 2 dusters in doing it. That's an enviable record, but better than that, it is money in the bank.

When I first met Mr. Hall, he was the senior partner of Hall & Briscoe. The story ran that Hall had started with $250 of his savings, even as I had done several times. The main difference was that he was cut out for a business man and I, for an airplane pilot. He went from one deal to another, with his working capital increasing at each change.

In following, or leading, the oil business in the midcontinent fields, Mr. Hall has been one of the greatest advocates of deep wells. It is his opinion that nearly all the dry holes drilled in oil-producing country can be made to give up the liquid gold, if they are drilled deep enough.

He has spent huge sums of money developing machinery to make such deep holes possible. Where a few years ago oil wells were averaging 2,500 to 3,000 feet in depth before the drillers gave up when no oil came forth, Mr. Hall's latest well was shot and brought in a gusher at nearly 7,500 feet. The courage it took to push the drills down that far at enormous daily costs is merely an example of his dogged determination and his consistency in following out his belief.

It was because Mr. Hall had a lot of faith in the plane,

and in Harold and me, that he helped us with the flight. He left to us everything in the matter of preparation and insisted that we pay for each detail with his money. I invested a little in special instruments and tools, but only a trifle compared to what Mr. Hall put up for us.

Mr. Hall has two hobbies—his daughter, Winnie Mae Fain, and aviation. Mrs. Fain used to ride all over with us in the Travelair. When I first knew her, she and Mr. Fain were living in Oklahoma City. Now they live in Long Beach, California, and they have a new baby that shows promise of becoming Mr. Hall's third hobby.

Mr. Hall has been like a second father to me. He knew how I had been injured in the drilling business. With a heart as big as his bank account and with Winnie Mae behind him, he bought that Travelair, and although he was a little squeamish about flying, his confidence in my meager ability as a pilot carried him through.

Cabin planes were improving every day, and the Hall family soon decided they were tired of getting all dressed up like magazine aviators just to travel a few hundred miles. So, late in 1928, my boss sent me out to the Lockheed factory in Los Angeles to turn in the Travelair for a new Lockheed Vega. I was overjoyed, for the new ship was to be one of those airplanes that could "go places and see things."

Mr. Hall told me to take plenty of time and to supervise closely the assembling of the Vega. He said that we should call it the "Winnie Mae" and have the name painted on the side.

Gradually the ship took shape. I was in constant touch, by telephone, with Oklahoma City, and I finally gained permission to go the limit on equipment. When the plane stood at the hangar door, ready for test flying, it was the most up-to-date airplane of 1928. The fourth Wasp-motored Lockheed, it was destined to carry the name "Winnie Mae" into first place wherever it went.

I had more pleasure test-flying that airplane than any of the dozens I have initiated to the air since. After Canucks, Jennies, and the Travelair, sitting at the stick behind that Wasp was like changing from a slow freight to a limited express. It was so sensitive and responsive to the controls that it seemed to anticipate my moves. And as for comfort—well, once one gets used to riding indoors, an open ship is just an old crate, no matter how good it may be otherwise.

Mr. Hall and Winnie Mae were just as happy as I was proud when I roared over the airport fence at Oklahoma City with the new ship. I pulled up in a steep climb to show off the tricks of the white bullet and then put her through her paces high in the air so that her new owner might see what a beautiful thing his "Winnie Mae" was.

I nearly got into trouble for that stunting. If I had had a license, I would have been grounded. But good old Oklahoma regarded pilots as good men who didn't need regulation, and I got away with the fancy show.

But after that, Mr. Hall insisted that "Winnie Mae" must conform to the regulations of the Department of Commerce, so I had to take out a pilot's license. That spelled trouble. My loss of an eye just about ruined my chances in the physical examination, but through Mr. Hall's intercession I was given a special dispensation. After a strict flying test and a set of written examinations, much more exacting than the customary tests for transport pilots, I was told that my license would be forthcoming as soon as I had flown 700 hours. Up to that time I had never kept a log book of my flying time, so I couldn't show any authentic record of the several thousand hours I had flown. I filled in the 700 hours within the following eight months and got my first license.

That was in the early fall of 1928. My employer was expanding his business of developing oil properties and had nearly all his available cash invested. The burden of carrying the plane and me along without giving us much work was beginning to seem heavy to him, so I tried to get him to let me take the ship for a try at some record.

I felt that I could get enough backing from commercial sources to finance the flight independently of Mr. Hall, and also that he would be pleased to have me take the plane off his hands temporarily. But as soon as he heard that I thought of letting commercial interests in on the flight (I hadn't decided yet just what flight I would make, but figured on a transcontinental record or a flight around the world), he vetoed the plan entirely. He had sunk some money in a couple of unsuccessful endurance flights, and he knew better than I how much special flights cost. He gave me some very good advice on not obligating myself. I am glad now that I took it.

Still, Mr. Hall had no particular need at that time for the "Winnie Mae." He was just about to take an offer for it from the factory in Los Angeles when I told him I wanted to fly the Pacific with it. Colonel William Easterwood, of Dallas, had offered a prize of $50,000 for a flight from Dallas to Hongkong. The conditions allowed for one stop for fuel, and with close figuring I at last worked out a schedule which the "Winnie Mae" might be able to make.

It was at that time that I first heard of Harold Gatty as a navigator. I bought Commander Weems' book on aërial navigation in anticipation of the Hongkong flight, and started studying. I also consulted the author, and he referred me to Gatty as his assistant and collaborator on the book.

Almost as soon as my plans were complete and I was getting ready for the final details, the $50,000 prize was taken down. I was sorely disappointed. I told Mr. Hall he had better sell the ship back to the Lockheed people after all, and I would deliver it to them. He decided to do so.

When I flew out to Los Angeles on what I thought was

a farewell trip in the "Winnie Mae," I unexpectedly ran into a job at the factory, as they needed a test pilot. They gave me a good raise in salary, and during the first part of 1929 I did all sorts of odd flying jobs. I went on a demonstration and sales tour through the northwestern cities of Washington and Oregon. Coming back to the factory, I did test flying and some experimental work. I learned a lot during that year, from drafting to actual aircraft design. Much of that knowledge stood me in good stead in preparing for my flight around the world, for many of the parts which give the second "Winnie Mae" extra speed and load are my own design.

Then I did some ferrying of ships. I didn't like that work because of the long train rides back. In the 1929 National Air Races, with the good old "Winnie Mae" again, I acted as escort for the women pilots in the Santa Monica-Cleveland derby. The race was won by Louise Thaden in a fast Travelair, and Amelia Earhart brought in the first Lockheed in third place.

When the Detroit Aircraft group took over the Lockheed plant, I was sent into the southwest to fly over an air line controlled by the parent company. I spent some time during the summer flying Lockheeds between El Paso and Brownsville, Texas, and Mazatlán, Mexico. I also flew in the 1929 National Air Tour for the Edsel B. Ford Reliability Trophy, and, although my ship made by far the fastest speeds of any of the planes in the tour, the formula on which the point score was based penalized the ship so that winning was impossible even before I started. But I had a lot of fun taking off last on 200-mile runs and getting in in first place.

Things went on about that way until June 5, 1930. I was a favored pilot in the crew of the Detroit Aircraft and got more good experience than I ever hope to get again. On that date, however, I got a call from my old employer, Mr.

Hall. "F. C." inquired about the "Winnie Mae" and was sorry to learn it had been sold by the factory. He ordered the name taken off the ship. It had already been painted out, much to my regret. I loved that old ship.

"If you can think of any improvements on a new 'Winnie Mae,' go ahead and get them," Mr. Hall said over the 'phone. "From now on you are working for me. I want a new ship, and I'll let you make some of those flights you were figuring on last year."

His tone surely made me put my heart into my work. I rushed into the main office and ordered a new ship. At first the engineers at the plant wanted to see a written order, but I finally overcame their scruples and got the work started.

It was a great day when the new "Winnie Mae" came off the line. She was about the last word in airplanes. I took her up on test and on bringing her back recommended a few changes. I wired Hall for permission to make them and got it without making any explanations. As soon as the changes were completed, I tore out of Los Angeles with Mrs. Post beside me and made the air hot with the skin friction of the wings, making tracks back to Oklahoma.

With a light heart I resumed my old duties as private pilot for the Hall family. Oklahoma and the people I knew so well looked good to me after so long an absence. I hardly got going, however, when the old desire to make a record flight took a tight hold on me again.

I planned a transcontinental flight. Mr. Hall passed on the plan, and I immediately jumped into preparation. Then some of my old business acumen, gained when I didn't have a Mr. Hall to pay the bills, came back. The management of the 1930 National Air Races at Chicago announced the non-stop derby for men between Los Angeles and Chicago. "Winnie Mae" was fast and had a good chance to win. What was to prevent winning that race, refueling, and getting away to New York immediately on the last leg of a transcontinental dash?

The answer was—nothing!

So I went about making more changes in the ship. I had the wing set at a little lower angle of incidence to lessen the resistant forces at high speeds. Knowing that I would have to land it with the tail well down, giving the wing a high angle of attack at slow speeds, I had 4 inches taken off the tail skid. This was to prevent the tail bouncing first on landings and tossing the ship over on its nose. I had tanks installed to bring the fuel capacity up to more than 500 gallons, and by the time I was through testing and adjusting the ship and engine, more than 10 miles an hour had been added to her originally fast top speed.

Then I went back to Gatty and got him to lay out a course for me. He worked all night before the start and pushed the maps and charts into my hand just before I took off. That was my first experience flying with accurate data of navigation, and it helped more than anything else. It won the race for me.

Misfortune prevented my transcontinental-record try on that trip. Running far ahead of my prearranged schedule, I had hopes of bringing the record down to less than 12 hours between Los Angeles and New York. Gatty's charts led me straight over the course, and my tail was being pushed along with a good wind. All of a sudden I saw my compass start swinging. Then it stuck. I had no other with me, so I had to navigate from the map. From Los Angeles to Chicago the course was 1,760 miles, and the details on the map were not very close together, although they looked very close on the state maps. I lost about 40 minutes on the flight. Even then, I still beat my nearest rival of the day into the field by 11 seconds. I had taken off half an hour later than he, which gave me a margin of that much more. The "Winnie Mae," off course and all, had averaged

192 miles an hour for the 1,760-mile direct course, and I think the record of 9 hours, 9 minutes and 4 seconds still stands between Los Angeles and Chicago.

I couldn't see how I could gas up the plane and get to New York in time to beat the 12 hour, 25 minute record set by Captain Frank Hawks. That loss of 40 minutes, due to a poor compass, ruined my chance to hold a real record that amounted to something in the United States. I abandoned the flight there in Chicago, satisfied to win the classic of the race meet and a $7,500 purse.

Next day I got a thrill. A plane like mine grew out of the west, took shape, and flashed across the finish line. The judges computed its time and declared it had beaten the plane which had followed me in to second place the day before. The new bidder for derby honors was Art Goebel, former holder of the transcontinental record. And what ship do you think he was flying?

Yes, sir! The old "Winnie Mae." Repainted a bit, slightly changed, and under a new boss, but still the good old airplane in which I had spent so many hours and on which many of my dreams were based.

Goebel and I compared notes and agreed that any airplane bearing the name "Winnie Mae" was destined to do great things. It was encouraging to know that a pilot as good as Art thought well of some of the ideas I had regarding Lockheeds.

When the final analysis of the derby came out, I discovered that Goebel had taken his navigation data from Gatty, also. That clinched the slight little Australian with me. He was going around the world with me, although he didn't know it at that time. I would take him if I had to shanghai him!

So that race will stick in my memory. The first two records for speed among all the fastest commercial airplanes in the country were held by "Winnie Mae's," and Harold Gatty set the courses for both of them.

I went back to Oklahoma and my duties as a pilot to the Hall family. I got a slight taste of being the returning hero when I landed in Chickasha, but I hope it didn't go to my head. Mr. Hall was so overjoyed at the performance of his new plane that he ordered me to go ahead with my around-the-world plan as fast as possible.

17

THE GATTY LOG

(GATTY)

SINCE THIS IS TO BE AN ACCOUNT OF MYSELF, I MAY AS WELL begin at the beginning. I am a native of Tasmania, one of those British colonies on which the sun never sets, according to legends drilled into my head in my early years of schooling in Zeehan. Like Wiley, I come from a large family, and responsibility thrust itself on me forcibly when I left the parental roof.

It was in Campbelltown, a medium-sized community, that I first saw the light of day, on January 5, 1903. My father, James Gatty, was a merchant who had come there from Australia, with my mother, the former Lucy Hall. I was the fifth child in the family.

When I was twelve years old, I won a scholarship by competitive examination and was transferred from the Zeehan grade school to St. Virgil's College at Hobart, one of the southernmost ports of the world. In the year spent in that institution I was much influenced by the sea and the odd-looking trading vessels which called at Hobart. I remember spending every available hour down by the docks, listening to the experiences and tales of the sailors. From the whalers to the windjamming lumber ships, every vessel fired my imagination.

The officers and rough seamen on those ships first gave me the ambition to sail the seas. Many of the adventurous yarns they spun were impossible of reënacting by the time I had completed my training and had become an officer on a regular ship. But it was the mysteries of the Antarctic as described by the whaling men, and the picturesque splendor as revealed in the stories of the oriental sailors that inspired me to compete a year later (1916) for entrance into the Royal Australian Naval College at Hobart. This institution corresponds to the Naval Academy at Annapolis. At that time there was a dearth of students as the War had taken most of the advanced classes to England. Under the circumstances, I had little trouble in being admitted.

The course was very thorough. I encountered most of my difficulties mastering mathematics. Strangely enough, that is my forte now. Part of my trouble in the beginning was that I was a romanticist. I used to find myself stranded on the ice-shelf edge of the Antarctic while the intricate problems of algebra were being explained in the classroom.

I put in three years and four months at the Naval College, making occasional visits home. My eldest brother, Leonard, had been killed at Gallipoli in 1915, but it was more than a year later that the sad news reached home. I was then the oldest living son, the other two older children being girls. They, too, had joined in war work. The elder, Doris, later settled in Hongkong, where she married an officer. The second, Dolly, went to England as a nurse and remained in London after the War.

It was only after much persuasion that I gained my parents' permission to follow my natural bent, the sea. The younger children of the house were still too small to be of much aid, aside from being a source of comfort to my mother. John was then only sixteen and Albert, the baby of the family, was fourteen.

As I had not been graduated from the Naval College, it was necessary for me to serve three years in apprenticeship before I would be eligible for my first examinations for a post and papers as fourth officer. The British Mercantile Marine is a hard school, but I was still anxious to follow the sea. After I had conclusively proved to my father that I had no aptitude for business, he finally consented to let me go on with my naval work.

With the certificate of his consent stowed away in the pocket of my best suit, I started back for Hobart in 1920, light-hearted and full of ambition. I signed my life away for the next three years and was placed with five other apprentices in service on a ship of the Patrick Steamship Company, Ltd. We plied between New Zealand, Tasmania, Australia, and the South Sea Islands, and my first impressions of those lands are among the most vivid memories of my life.

I never got tired of visiting port, but the work on board was grueling. As apprentices, young men are put through the hardest work on the boat. We had to do as much or more work than the able seamen—act as supercargo, stand watch with the officers, and run their errands—all in addition to completing a course of study in ship navigation and operation.

For one weak in mathematics, my own course was tough to plot. I had to overcome my aversion to figures before I made any headway. My companions did more for me than anything else. They destroyed my illusions, one after another, and brought the world to me in cold hard facts, so that my mind no longer wandered into infinite space when the figures on the paper blurred before my sight in the late hours of the night. There was no time for colorful sea tales on merchant vessels after the War, and gradually my imagination stagnated. (Since leaving the sea, however, it has somewhat revived, and some day I hope to go back and live the life I first dreamed of living in the out-of-the-way ports of the South Seas.)

I showed a great proficiency in languages and was picked by my five companions to do all the talking on our visits in ports where English was not spoken. Those five lads were wild, though, and my responsibility as spokesman often got me into trouble. They were usually planning some practical joke on me or on some poor shopkeeper, and naturally, having given the orders, I was held to blame. Two or three times the captain was called on to get me out of difficulty, and that made my troubles worse. I couldn't afford to tell on my companions or my life aboard would have been made unbearable, so I had to stand the gaff for the whole crew of us. But those five were a great set and made it up to me in other ways. Before we were out three months, we had formed a sort of pact—"one for five and five for one," to paraphrase the slogan of the Dumas Musketeers.

The engineer's side of the seafaring profession never interested me. A certain amount of training in the motive-power and maintenance divisions of the steamship line was a necessary part of my curriculum as apprentice, but I never could become absorbed in it. I suppose my imagination was appealed to by the stars and moon, which play so important a part in navigation. I used to lie in a hammock on deck, just behind the forecastle, in order to study late at night. Light came over my shoulders from the windows of the galley where the cook and mess help were cleaning up after the evening meal.

When the light went out, I would continue to lie there and pick out my favorite stars. I soon reached the stage where I could tell time by the relative positions of the various solar groups. I learned the changes in their positions in the various seasons of the year, and from a few old books on Greek and more ancient folklore, picked up in Sydney, I gleaned the legends connected with the more important constellations.

My interest in the stars and the solar system is hard for anybody to understand who has not seen the ceiling of the South Seas on a clear night. Nowhere have I seen its equal for splendor, brilliance, or clearness. Quite aside from its effect on an impressionable mind, I feel that it is the finest possible school for stellar instruction.

All too soon my three-year term as apprentice came to an end. I took my fourth mate's papers after an examination in Hobart where I had first learned the rule of the sea. I specialized in navigation, and got through the tests with flying colors.

Then to my first job. That was a problem of no mean proportions to a newly made sailorman. My best bet was Sydney, so to Sydney I went on the first ship. I invaded the office of one of the largest steamship companies in the world, the Union S. S. Company of New Zealand, and put in my application. Once connected with that line, one was practically certain of a lifetime place. The order of seniority was strictly observed in promotions, and no ship's officer was ever demoted. One would go from fourth mate on a big boat to third mate on a smaller vessel. Then to a similar post on a larger ship, and so on, until the final promotion brought one to a captaincy. It was a long road but straight, sure, and adventurous.

I went to a rooming house I had formerly patronized when in port on my earlier voyages, prepared to wait indefinitely for an appointment. Next morning I was more than surprised when my landlady awakened me and delivered a message from the line. It ordered me to report for duty immediately.

At that time, the line had more than seventy ships in

regular service, and its business covered the entire Pacific Ocean, the Indian Ocean, the ports of Africa, and around Good Hope to the British Isles. The ships carried both passengers and freight, depending on which service they were in, and a schooling as part of the personnel of the fleet was as thorough as could be had anywhere in the world.

My first assignment was aboard the "Maleno," a combination passenger-and-freight carrier between Sydney and New Zealand. The whole episode is forcibly impressed on my mind because of a strange occurrence which happened the night I filed my application with the company.

At my rooming house I met a traveling violinist who forecast my future for me. I have never been a great believer in mysticism, fortune-telling, or any of the kindred arts, but during the next five years the prophecies of that violinist turned out to be absolutely accurate. Without knowing who I was, or that I had filed that application, he told me that I was to go away on the morrow for a long trip.

Then, I attributed that "guess" to his powers of observation, for one glance at my wind-wrinkled and tanned faced showed that I was a sailor. Any lingering doubt would have been banished by his watching my walk. But he also predicted I would be gone exactly a year. He said that I would visit the United States and get ahead in whatever profession I followed. That I would abandon one calling for another, marry, and have three children. All that information came to me entirely unsolicited. I took the trouble to write down much of the conversation with the violinist as soon as I signed on the ship.

One year later—to the day—I landed again in Sydney. I was there to assume a new post as third mate on a tanker, the "Orowaiti." Again I met the violinist. He was on the street near the wharf, where he earned a bare living fiddling for the seamen in a café.

My tanker was soon afterward taken from service in New Zealand waters and sent to San Luis Obispo on the coast of California. That was my promised visit to the United States. Gradually the idle prophecies of the violinist seer were coming true.

My first impressions of this great country were highly absurd. We landed just at dusk. One of my shipmates, a member of the original group of apprentices, and I hired an old Ford to go to Pismo Beach where a carnival was in progress. Of course, we had heard tales of the United States from seamen and officers—that the streets were paved with gold, that the life was rough, the tempers quick, and that anything from gambling to arson and murder "went."

That carnival, except for the last two crimes mentioned, seemed to justify the stories that had been told me. I invaded the dance pavilion and was still there at midnight, when my companions said to stand by, that it was time to leave for the ship, which was scheduled to sail for Australia in the morning. I had one more dance and rushed out. There was the old Ford, disappearing in a cloud of dust.

I was in a sorry predicament. It had been a custom with me, as with my shipmates, never to return to ship from leave with a single ha'penny, or whatever the smallest coin of the realm happened to be. So now I was not only left behind, but was penniless as well.

I looked through the crowd for a friendly face, but I saw that the people were too busy enjoying themselves to be bothered with a lone sailor. Earlier in the evening I had watched a pair rough-up a panhandler who was trying to earn his beer by telling a sad tale of woe, so I didn't dare try that as I was only five feet five and pretty light for my height.

There seemed to be nothing to do but to walk back to the ship, which I thought must be about twenty miles away. With malice in my heart for Pat Collings, my former apprentice companion who, I felt sure, was responsible for my plight, I started dragging my weary feet shipward.

On the way down I had noticed that the road curved far inland and then back again to shore. So I decided to take what looked like a short cut through a cañon.

After walking about two and a half hours, I was completely lost in one of those dense California land fogs. Aimlessly I roamed on. My whole career was at stake, the career for which I had been studying and working for the past eight years. Dawn broke over the edge of some cliffs, just as the sea came within hearing, lashing against the base of the rocks. I found that I was on a ledge and might have walked over the side at any step for some distance back. The cañon ended there at the edge of the Pacific.

With great exertion I climbed the side of the rockbound ravine and found the highway. It ran east and west, and at first I didn't know which way to go on it. I feared it might be just a byroad leading out to some resort on the shore.

A lone hobo came trudging along, and from him I got directions to San Luis Obispo. I ran, walked, scurried, and finally stumbled into sight of the wharf just in time to jump aboard the tanker before it backed out into the channel.

Truly, my first impressions of the United States were mixed, but later visits so charmed me that I have already taken out first papers and hope to be a bona fide citizen within the next few years.

Meanwhile, my study of navigation was advancing, and I could hit the course on the dot and on schedule on most of the voyages. I had several new ideas which were frowned upon by the masters of the various ships on which I worked as navigating officer. However, I plotted the course from new formulae I had worked out, and then made out my reports by the conventional methods.

My first big test came when I was third mate on the steamer "Wahine," in passenger service over a 210-mile run between Nelson and Wellington, New Zealand, across Cook Strait. The ship was very fast (21 knots), and the weather in that strait is bad. Fogs roll out from the land and cover the channels, reducing visibility to zero in half an hour.

This night, one of my first trips on the route, the captain retired almost as soon as we cleared the port on the south side of the strait. Just before he left me in charge on the bridge he spoke of the speed of the ship and impressed on me the great responsibility I had in caring for the safety of the sleeping passengers.

Less than half an hour later the fog began to roll toward the ship. From the bridge I saw it coming—a great, yawning blackness on the horizon. Before I knew it, I couldn't see the forecastle directly ahead.

I was scared.

I had the 'phone in my hand to call the captain for orders when the first mate appeared on the bridge. He was a kindly man and a good superior officer. He warned me not to call the skipper.

"If you do, and the ship gets through, you admit your inability to navigate. If you get the old man out and he doesn't get through, he will 'pass the buck' back to you. But if you try to pull her through yourself, the chances are that you will, and that you'll earn a promotion in the bargain," he said.

I thanked him, and he went below. I still think he kept a sharp watch, but if he did, he never mentioned it. I held my breath, or so it seemed, for the next hour. At last I got used to seeing nothing ahead, and toward the end of the watch I was reluctant to turn the post over to my relief.

When I returned to the bridge again shortly after 8 A.M., I found that the fog had begun to break up forty minutes after midnight and had burned away completely a few hours after dawn, which comes early down there at that time of year. The third mate, who relieved me at midnight, said that he had continued to follow the same course and drift allowance which I had plotted during the thick fog and had turned over to him when I went off watch. As the ship neared port directly on her course, the episode was a source of great satisfaction to me.

My long-cherished desire to find adventure on the sea gradually waned as modern transportation invaded the remote waterways of the South Seas, and I became accustomed to the precision of the mechanical contrivances of navigation.

The final demise of my ambition to imitate the heroes of Conrad, McFee, and other chroniclers of sea tales, was hastened by my frequent visits to Sydney. Each time I arrived there, I called at the home of James McColloch, a shipbuilder, whose reputation as a steelworker was famous in the dry docks. Jim listened to my queries with regard to new developments in ship design with his tongue in his cheek, and then went out. So his daughter Vera and I were naturally thrown a great deal in each other's company. I found her much more interesting than the new keels which were being laid at her father's yard.

To make matters worse for my career at sea, it was spring on one of my visits to Sydney, and I allowed my thoughts to run with Tennyson. The upshot and conclusion of the matter was a wedding and a resolution to be quit of the roving life of the sailor. That was on June 3, 1925. Times were hard in Australia then, and I was forced to put in two years at sea after that.

Almost immediately after our marriage Mrs. Gatty and I had made application for entrance into the United States under the quota regulations. Immigration from Australia was restricted, and it took the full two years before our numbers were approved by the consulate. Meanwhile, we had become three, and Alan, born on May 20, 1926, was more than a year old.

The problem which confronted me then was much more difficult than any I had had in navigation, for in the latter study I was daily becoming more proficient, according to the captain. I considered many devious ways of circumventing the desire of the American consul to separate me from my family by making my son immigrant No.— in my stead and leaving me behind, a British seaman. With his assurance that another application would be quickly approved, I consented at last to let Mrs. Gatty and the boy enter California on the first two numbers. Once more I took a post on the old tanker "Orowaiti," the ship in which I first had visited the United States. I signed up for one voyage, and waited for the approval of my application to follow my family to the United States.

Two months later I left the sea for good, resigning from the company. My officer's papers were valid only on ships of English registry, which precluded my entering the mercantile service of my adopted country. I filed my first papers for United States citizenship the first possible moment after my arrival in Los Angeles.

Then I had to find some way in which I might fit into the new life in America. Unfortunately for me, I knew but one thing—the sea and its ways. After spending some time seeking employment in vain, I was in despair. I picked up odd jobs along the water front, compensating compasses, plotting courses for sportsmen who owned yachts, and writing a few articles on navigation. Later I worked as instrument adjuster on the planes at the airport.

A windfall came to me when Dr. Donald Dickey helped me get a mate's post on Keith Spalding's yacht "Goodwill." Mr. Spalding was a wealthy sportsman who was planning a four-month cruise in the Pacific and needed an experienced navigator. I learned a lot of American customs and business requirements on that cruise while the yacht was riding anchor among the fishing banks in the Gulf of California, so that when I was through with the assignment I knew better how to go about my search for permanent employment.

Interest in aviation along the Pacific Coast was running high in 1928. The Dole race and the flight of Maitland and Hegenberger to Hawaii were inducing flyers to seek more distant goals.

On investigation I found that few pilots knew much of navigation other than flying by map. This situation promised some employment, and I began instructing flyers in navigation from the sailor's viewpoint instead of from the railroad outlook they were used to. Even the military pilots, whose training was as complete as that given by any flying school in the world, were lacking in the knowledge of navigation.

Gradually my small school began to attract a little attention. Commander P. V. H. Weems—a navigator of great renown and a scientist as well—became one of my friends. With years of experience in the navy, he quickly realized that the aviation industry of the future must have a navigation system of its own to offset the variations between flying and all other forms of transport, variations which magnified the minute errors which can be disregarded on steamships.

My student body in the school was always small, but among the names on the roll were several well-known pilots. Art Goebel was one of my first pupils. As one pilot would finish the course, his friends would come for tutoring, and while the time was not yet ripe for the universal education of pilots as finished navigators, still I managed to keep going. Flyers who were planning long flights and were in need of aid in plotting courses provided me with employment, and soon I had to hire an assistant to take care of the school.

One day Harold Bromley called on me and wanted to be tutored to navigate a course from Tacoma, Washington, to Tokyo, Japan. I divided my time between that job and collaborating with Commander Weems in the assembling of a great mass of data he had collected, from which he was evolving what is now known as the "Weems' System of Aërial Navigation." This method obviates the use of mathematical computations in flight, and by means of tables made by Commander Weems after an exhaustive study greatly simplifies getting a position. He used a "star-curve" chart in plotting the formulae from which the figures on the tables were calculated, and I applied myself to the detail work of solving the equations.

Then we tried to devise instruments which would be calibrated in accordance with the tables. In a few instances we succeeded. The most successful of these instruments are a positive-drift indicator, a ground-speed indicator, and a watch dial which simplifies the conversion of local, Greenwich civil, Greenwich apparent, and Greenwich star times.

Although Bromley cracked up his airplane on his start from Tacoma, he stuck doggedly to his resolution and asked me to go to Japan with him as soon as he could get a new ship which would carry two persons. We were to fly the originally planned course but in the reverse direction, and he wanted me along as navigator. The flight promised some reward, as several cash prizes had been posted for the first person to fly between the United States and Japan.

But I had a distinguished student, Mrs. Charles A. Lindbergh, whom I was tutoring in navigation, and several others were waiting for me to find time to give them private instruction. There is a self-consciousness about experienced pilots which prevents them from registering in open classes, and my time was in demand giving private lessons in elementary phases of course-plotting and -altering, and other problems in navigation.

But at last I agreed to go with Bromley, and we packed, on the deck of a Dollar liner, the Lockheed monoplane he had equipped for the flight back. After some delay and a change in the point first planned for the take-off, we bounded into the air on September 14, 1930, and nosed out over the Pacific with Seattle as our goal. Some ten hours later we picked up a thick fog and started through it, but when our engine began to heat up, we suddenly wheeled the ship about and back-tracked as fast as we could fly to Japan. We did manage to keep the engine going until we arrived at the starting point again. Then we were almost sorry we hadn't kept on.

Soon afterward the flight ran out of backing, and we returned to California. With a second son, Lindsay, born May 21, 1928, and a third son, Ronald, born the following year, I was glad that we hadn't chanced the continuation of the flight after the engine lost some of its power.

From my experience with Bromley I had learned some of the technical obstacles to long-distance flights, and I began to think aëronautically. I resumed my work tutoring embryo navigators and "experting" on instruments. My services to pilots improved, and nearly all of those landing at Lindbergh Field came in to see me at some time or other during the next few months, while I was instructing there. Then I formed the alliance with Wiley Post to beat the record of the "Graf Zeppelin" and plunged into the preparations for that, as I have already related.

L' ENVOI

(GATTY)

WILEY AND I WOULD MUCH RATHER FLY THAN WRITE ABOUT flying. The technical knowledge gained from our flight, outlined in the foregoing chapters, will some day, we hope, be applied to commercial transport.

How well we proved our points can only be determined by future operations of aircraft. With superlative "stick technique" Post dispelled the bugbear of all flyers, the fear that one cannot fly blind for any appreciable length of time. He made good his boast and theory that the airplane can be flown farther, faster, and cheaper than any other form of air transport.

For my part, I feel that the precision with which "Winnie Mae" was able to hold her course is adequate proof that the finer points which distinguish aërial navigation from the older methods of the mariner are well worth the time and money which the aircraft industry has expended in their development.

Otherwise, the only thing left to say is what a famous

and much-sought-after but publicity-shy flyer said when asked what he thought of a recent flight. Somewhat nonplussed, he remarked:

"Aviation *must* be making great strides. And *that*, my friend, is for publication."

Log Book

ROUND-THE-WORLD FLIGHT
OF THE "WINNIE MAE"
(Pilot: Wiley Post; navigator: Harold Gatty)

Publisher's Note: On the following pages are reproduced exact facsimiles of the pages of the *Log Book* kept by Harold Gatty during the flight of the "Winnie Mae."

In this log Mr. Gatty used a 24-hour day as a basis of his time entries, except that in noting the time of arrival at Berlin he entered the time on a 12-hour basis; that is, as 7:30 rather than 19:30.

New York – Harbour
Tuesday June 23rd

Time	Position or Locality	M.C.	Ground speed	Altitude	R.P.M	Air temp	Oil temp	thro tem
June GCT			S. m.					
23 8.55 21	Roosevelt field	63°						
9.24	Guilford 2ml		138					
9.35				2000	1725	60	70	40
9.50			150					
9.53½	Woonsocket 2ml							
10.04	over Boston	38						
10.20	Newbury port (over)							
10.30		38	150	1200	1700	57	68	40
10.47	Portland	90						
11.15			150					
12.00			165	800	1710	60	69	39
13				400	1720	66	70	45
14.03	R. Piney		170					
14.30								
15.00			180					
15.42	Harbour Grace							

Grace

AIR SPEED	WIND	Drift	Remarks
			took off 4.55 DST Sk. Visibility poor.
		0	9.30 Sky clearing
41		oil press 85	
	light NE	0	
			10.07 a/c 38° (M)
			10.28½ Portsmouth (maine) over
40		oil press 84	10.41½ Biddeford (over)
	NW	4°R	a/c 82° (C)
	NW	4°R	a/c 78°
42			oil Press 84
43			" " 83 Air very rough.
		15°R	a/c
		10°R	
			15.00 Passed over french territory
			little & Grand miquelon
			15.42 Arrived Harbour Grace
			Av. speed from New York 168.3 mph

Harbour Grace —

Date	Time GCT	Position or Locality	M.C	Ground Speed	Altitude	R.P.M.	Air Temp.	Oil Temp	He To
June 23th	19 25	Harbour Grace		170					
	20 00				800				
	20.25	No 2		170	500				
	21.30				1800				
	21.55	No 3		170					
	22.00	Posn by obser			1600	1450	60	69	H
	22 23	51°N 42°W	moon & sun lines fix.						
	23.15								
June 24	00 32	No 5							
	1.00								
	1.30								
	4.25								
	11.42	Irish Coast							
	17.00	Landed Berlin							

Barrèn

D	Wind	Drift	Remarks
	NW	2° R	Took 1/4 19.25 %c 89½(m) strong fell wind cloudy
	SW	5 L	
	SW	9° L	20.25 %c 94° (NOIC) overcast hazy
	SSW	12 L	
S			
S			oil pressure 85
			23.15 %c 88° mag
			00.32 %c 100° (No 1 C)
			Flying blind
			ditto
			"
			4.25 %c 105½° (mag)

Berlin —

Date June	Time GCT	Position or Locality	T.C	M.C	Ground speed	Altitude	R.P.M	Air Temp	Oil Temp	
	6.35	Took off Tempelhof T/C								
	6.38									
	7.04½	Custrin		73°	151	2000				
	4.19	3 W Landsberg		"						
	7.51½	Schindermull								
	8.32	Schwetz								
	8.41	Riesenburg								
	13.30			79°						
26	14.40									
	2.01	Moscow								
	3.21	Oka River								
	3.29	Volga River		83						
	4.00	" "		97°	152	3000		80°		
	4.52	Kazan		70°						
	6.03	Sarapul								
	8.34	Shadrinsk	100°	11°E	90°					
	9.04	Tobol River over								
	11.00	Omsk	88	10°	79					
	13.32	Subinsk								

Speed	Wind	Drift	Remarks
			6.35 Took off from Tempelhoff Aerodrome
			6.38 ⁹/c 75 (m)
			7.04½ Over Custrin a Oder + Wartha Rivers
			overcast low clouds rain
			10.34 Passed Vilna 6.m R.
			11.24 Crossed border Poland a USSR
			12.00 Heavy rain – hedge hopping no visibility
			1.20. Still rain + more rain Strong head winds. Toughest part of the flight so far.
N			14.40 Landed Moscow
			2.01 Took off from Moscow S/c 78½ (m). for Kazan.
			3.21 Crossed Oka River
			3.29¼ 83° m.c. Volga River 4' left.
S	3L		over Kazan ⁹/c 67° (No 1 cc)
			" Sarapul ⁹/c 70° (C)
			Shadrinck 4ᵐ R.
			11.00 Over Omsk on Irtish River S/c 79°(mag) for Novo Sibirsk
			13.32 Arrived at Novo Sibirsk

Novo Sibirsk — Irkutsk

Date	Time GCT	Position or Locality	T.C	M.C	Ground Speed	Altitude	R.P.M	Air Temp	Oil Temp	
26	21.47	Novo Sibirsk	80°	71°						
	23.24	over Lake Shanpor	72°	64°		4000				
24th	00.14	over Krasnoyarsk								
	00.37	50'past "	119½°	115½°						
	3.50	Iskuiell								
	6.09	Irkutsk	91	91¼						
	6.35	Lake Baikal								
	7.25	Kurba River								
	7.43				98°	161				
	8.42	over Chita			100°					
	9.10				104					
	10.29	Amur River								
	13.00	Landed Blagoveshchensk								
28th	1.21	Blago								
	3.56	Khabarovsk								

— Khabarovsk.

R	Wind	Drift	Remarks

21.45 Took off Novo Sibirsk (H.45 L.CT)
21.47 ¾c 80°T. 69° Mag.
Cloudy passing showers low haze.
Rugged country thick forest
Lake Sharipoo ¾c 64° Mag.
23.55 flying over thick cloud layer
24. Now under — over the tree tops
tough going through the mountains
00.14 Krasnoyarsk. across Yenisei River
more rain + low flying similar to
Berlin — Moscow flight.
3.50 Landed Irkutsk
6.09 Took off from Irkutsk
6.10 ¾c 84° (C) 6.35 crossed western
6.44½ crossed eastern shore Lake Baikal
    High mountains + flat grassy valleys
7.25 Crossed Kurka River   Airspeed 161
4.43 ¾c 94° (C)
8.28½ over Bklamish a lakes
8.42 Chita ¾c 96° (C)
9.01 ¾c 100° (C)
10.29 Crossed Amur River into Manchuria

1.21 Took off from Blagoveshchensk

3.56 Landed Khabarovsk

Date	Time G.C.T.	Position or Locality	T.C	M.C	Ground speed	Altitude	R.P.M	Air Temp	Oil Temp	Sha Temp
June 29		(7 Pm Local Time) Took off from Khabarovsk			140					
	8.56		0							
"	8.58		52							
			''							
		Amur River	ᒐ							
			ᒐ							
			—ᒐ—							
	11.39	Left Amur River	(52) 52	140						
	12.12	W coast Saghalin (62°C)								
	13.25	N o 3		59°		1500				
	15.03	N O 4								
	15.25	N O 4	62½(E)			6000		46		
	16.00									
	17.40	N o 6								
30 "	1.48	Landed Solomon								

Nome

Wind	Drift	Remarks

LN

8.56 Took off from Khabarousk 5mi wide
8.58 S/c 50°(C) down Amur River
Flying low about 75ft over river & marshes.
clear weather.
10.00 Passed paddle Steam going down Amur
10.03 Passed Orloubkoe 4 m R
10.16. High hills flying over treetops
10.25 Along the river scaring the natives
          in their sampans.

N

10.47. Kargo 2 m R   10.55 Sunset
Wind North abt 8 mph.

11.39 Left Amur River 1/c 54°(C) dark

ESE 8°L

8L 13.25 Nos position 1/c 89° mag
5L 15. Hard Flying   down

16.00 Heavy rain Flying blind.
16.30 Still blind
17.20 In and above fog

Date	Time G.C.T.	Position or Locality	T.C.	M.C	Ground Speed	Altitude	R.P.m	Air Temp	Oil Temp	Tho Tm
30 1	4.20	Solomon (Nome)		68(C)						
1	7.26	Fairbanks								
	13.25	Fairbanks								
	17.13	Quet Lake	110°	76°						
	21.30	Peace River								
	23.30	Edmonton								

via Fairbanks

. D	Wind	Drift	Remarks
			4.20 Took off from Nome (Solomon Beach) & S/c 68° (C) for Fairbanks. more fog flying on top.
	direct		Route along the Yukon & Tenana rivers.
			7.26 Landed Fairbanks.
			13.25 Took off from Fairbanks for Edmonton 15.00 Crossed border Yukon & Alaska 15.15 " White River 16.36 Crossed Yukon River 50 No/E of Whitehorse 17.13 Passed S. edge Dluet Labe S/c 76° mag
			Heavy rain flying low
			23.30 Landed Edmonton

Date	Time G.C.T	Position or Locality	T.C.	m.c	Ground Speed	Altitude	R.P.m	Air Temp.	Oil Temp	He... Te...
July 1st	10.37	Edmonton		$83\frac{1}{2}°$						
"	12 20½	Saskatoon		84°(C)						
	16.58	Lake Superior								
	1905	Lake Michigan								
	21.15	Cleveland								
	21.45	Cleveland		99°						
	22 55			108°						
2nd	2304½	Bellefonte		$99\frac{1}{2}°$						
2	00.25	New Brunswick								

Wind	Drift	Remarks

10.37 Took off Edmonton
10.38 3/c 8 315° Mag
overcast & rain

11.43 following wind

12 20½ Saskatoon 1ᵐ R.

10° 12.50

13.31 Yorktown 2ᵐ R
weather clearing

16.58 Crossed W shore Lake Superior
17.24   "   E   "   "   "
19 05 Crossed E shores Lake Michigan

21.15 landed Cleveland

21.45 took off from Cleveland for New York
22 55 Clairfield 1ᵐ R
00.25 New Brunswick N J
0 47 landed R. Field